The Return of an Ancient Partner

HEMP

Design, layout, and printing by
Morris Press
a division of Morris Printing Group, Kearney, Nebraska

D1708608

TABLE OF CONTENTS

TABLE OF CONTENTS

Hemp
The Return of an Ancient Partner

Hemp, one of the very first cultivated crops, has played an important role in human history for thousands of years. Hemp sails, rigged with hemp rope, pushed explorers and armadas around the globe - sometimes to glory and sometimes to disaster. With its valuable seed and oil, its usefulness as a medicinal herb and religious artifact, and with its superior fiber for paper, textiles and rope, the hemp plant was a cultural and economic powerhouse for 10,000 years. With an unmatched ability to adapt to local growing conditions, hemp joined humans in their march across the globe.

Unfortunately, eighty years ago the United States pushed hemp into the ditch with misguided and unjustified prohibition. But today hemp is regaining its status as one of our most useful natural resources. Like corn and soybeans, hemp is now grown for an expanding menu of food and industrial purposes. Hemp seed, composed of 45 percent oil, 35 percent protein and 10 percent carbohydrates and fiber, has a robust nutritional future. Hemp oil, traditionally used for industrial functions such as paint and varnish, is now finding major new markets in the cosmetic and food industries. The CBD compounds in hemp are now being evaluated for a host of medicinal uses. New uses for hemp fibers are being created in the drive for sustainable economic development.

In 1938, *Popular Mechanics* magazine discussed the future of hemp in a feature article, declaring it the "new billion dollar crop." The next few years will see that prediction come true, and will see the full return of our ancient partner. This book celebrates that return.

MY HISTORY WITH HEMP

My Father's Mother stayed on the farm,
Rooted tough as an Osage Orange.
There was hemp in the draw,
And dabbed along the fence line,
And a bit down along the creek.

Grandma didn't cut the hemp,
She left it for the birds.
The home covey paid with a parade of chicks.
Bobwhites, with their two note call
And a royalty of feathers.

A limestone ledge on the Eighty
Dared a young boy and the cousins to jump.
The Forty held an arrowhead for a sharp eye.
Grandma drove the tractor, we threw the hay bales
In the race with the rain to the barn.

There was hemp in the draw, and
Lord! The doves loved it!
Sometimes with Dad's shotgun they were our supper.
Get ready boys, this might be a double.
Dad and Jim fire together, grey birds tumble.

Grandma fought the thistle,
But she didn't cut the hemp.
She knew it couldn't get you high.
She hated Johnson grass and bindweed, who didn't?
But hemp was good for the farm.

By: Allan Jenkins

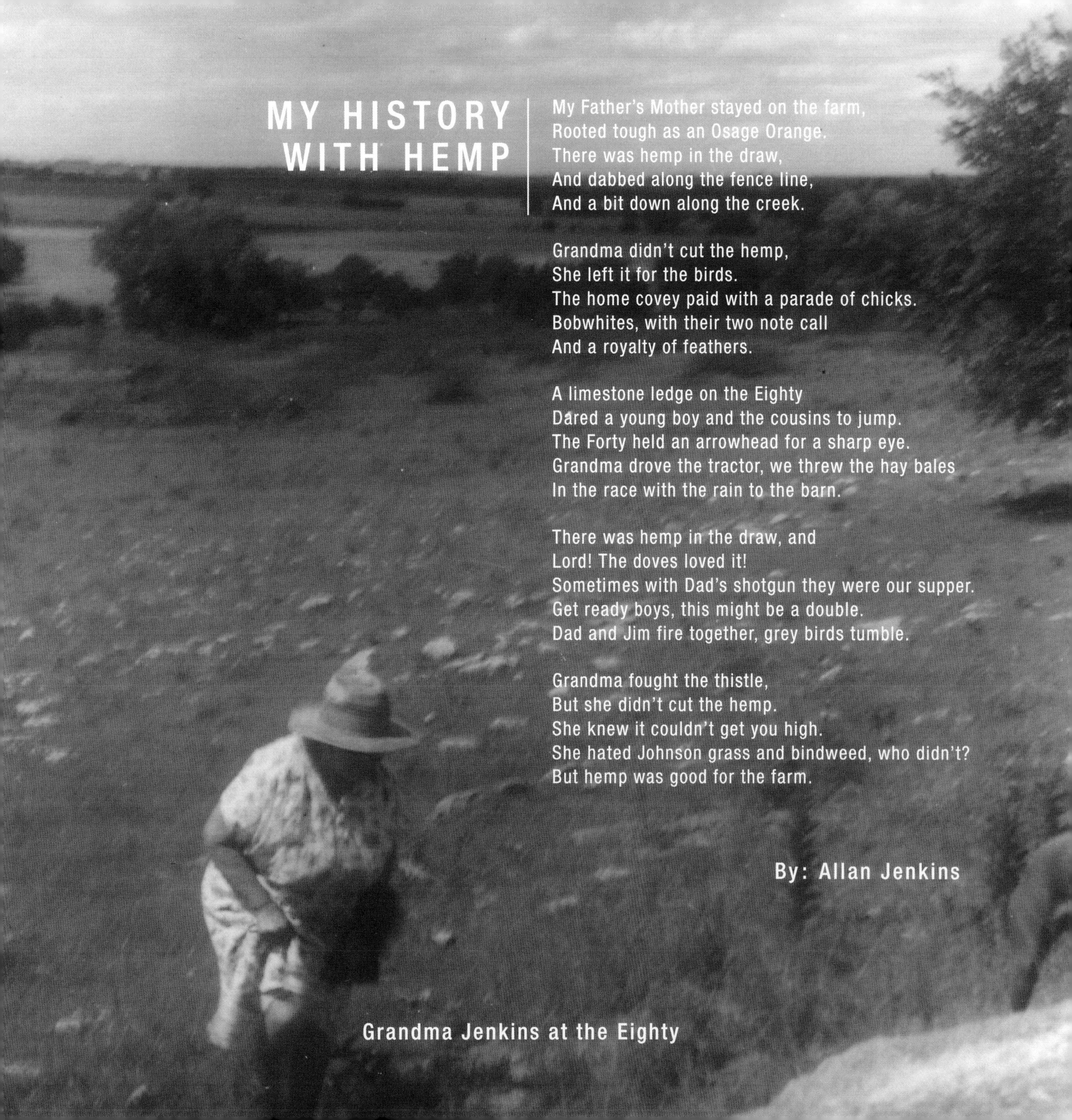

Grandma Jenkins at the Eighty

Experimental hemp crop in Colorado, Colorado State University

Humans and Hemp
{First Encounters and Cultivation}

As modern humans moved out of Africa 85,000 years ago, they crossed the mouth of the Red Sea and slowly moved along the coast of the Arabian Peninsula. With movement came risk and reward - each new territory might host a bounty of usable resources, or might hold starvation and death. The risks were real, the first attempted migration out of Africa 40,000 years earlier had ended in disaster along the eastern shores of the Mediterranean. It appears that the second wave reduced its risk by staying close to the food resources of the ocean, taking 10,000 years to reach the southern tip of India. Another 10,000 years, and the migrants had looped around Borneo and reached southern China. Successful hunter-gatherer clans were adaptive and innovative as they slowly spread north, learning to use the indigenous plants and animals they encountered. When the hunter-gatherers reached the Yangtze River basin they found a great diversity of wild game, nuts, grasses, berries, and edible roots. This was an area of seasonal monsoon rainfall, with hot summers and cool to cold winters. There were large swaths of fertile windblown loess soils and shallow lakes, the residual of glacial activity in central Asia during the Pleistocene Age. For 40,000 years, each generation lived a subsistence lifestyle like their ancestors - although unpredictable changes in weather and rainfall patterns, and the resulting relative abundance or scarcity of game animals and food plants, created year-to-year challenges.

A seismic change in lifestyle came to the Yangtze Valley 10,000 to 12,000 years ago when the local inhabitants began to purposefully cultivate one widely occurring indigenous plant - rice (*Oryza sativa L.*). The cultivated rice was one of many wild and weedy rice forms which naturally grew in present-day southern China, India, and Indochina. The Yangtze Valley was located near the northern boundary of naturally occurring rice, which may have contributed to the initial decision by the locals to try to increase the supply of the desirable grain by purposefully helping it grow. The hunter-gathers must have noticed the conditions which provided plentiful wild rice in some years and minimal yields in other years. Desiring the grain, they began to create the conditions favorable for rice growth.

Rice cultivation provided a stable food supply allowing increased human population and the beginnings of permanent settlements. Other crops, like foxtail millet and broomcorn millet were soon planted. The domestication of goats, chickens and pigs quickly followed the emergence of crop cultivation. As the early farmers purposefully altered the local environment to increase crop production and increase vegetative feed for their domesticated animals, they were inadvertently creating conditions conducive to the growth of another indigenous Asian plant - hemp (*Cannibis sativa L*).

Current thought is that hemp first evolved on the steppes of Central Asia or along the eastern edge of the Himalayas. By the time of modern human migration, wild hemp was growing across central Asia, in the Caspian Basin, and in the foothills of the Himalayas. Hunter-gatherers had to successfully exploit the local environment to survive, so they were continually testing new plants that they encountered as they slowly moved into new territory. When they first encountered hemp on their migration, they surely discovered the seeds were edible and the plant produced long, strong fibers.

The beginnings of agriculture in the Yangtze Valley would have quickly pulled hemp into the early fields. Hemp favors nutrient dense soils, so the manure-rich environment created by the early farmers with their herds of domesticated animals provided ideal growing conditions. Because many birds feed on hemp seeds, wild strains would have naturally found their way to areas cleared by animal grazing or crop cultivation. The recognized value of the seeds, oils and fibers quickly convinced farmers to purposefully plant hemp, thus making it one of the very first cultivated crops. Early Asian farmers valued hemp because of its versatility and hardiness. The seed could be used for food or oil, but early Chinese cultivation was focused on producing hemp for fiber. Hemp has two separate fibers - an outer bast that is long and strong and an inner hurd that is softer and pulpy. Hemp textiles made from the bast are strong, and provided an outstanding choice for rough clothes and rope.

The archaeological record for plants is always problematic, and it is unlikely that we will ever know exactly when and where in Asia hemp was first purposefully grown. For some plants, botanists can estimate the area and time of domestication by charting the genetic characteristics of plant variants relative to their geographic

Male & Female Hemp Plants

Hemp Breaking

distribution over time. However, the hemp plant is characterized by rapid and radical change in response to new environments. Further, domesticated hemp easily cross-pollinates with wild versions of the plant. This tangles the genetic pathway, making it impossible to work backward to find an original site. Though unable to identify a point of origin, we know without a doubt that hemp was one of the first cultivated crops. Researchers have found traces of hemp cord dating back 10,000 years in present-day China and Taiwan and further evidence of early hemp use across the region and into Tibet by 5,000 B.C. Hemp textiles were widely spread across northern China 4,500 years ago.

Hemp's natural characteristics greatly aided its rapid geographical advance. The plant rapidly acclimates to a variety of growing environments, has few natural pests, and crowds out most weeds. Hemp is dioecious, meaning there are separate male and female plants. Male plants are tall and thin, with pods containing the fertilizing, pollen-generating stamen. The female plant, darker and shorter, has short hairs protruding to capture pollen. Wind-assisted pollination can originate with a male plant several miles from the female. With each female plant producing thousands of seeds transported by wind, water and wildlife, hemp is a naturally aggressive wild colonizer. Wind blown pollen and thousands of seeds per female plant creates a recipe for rapid natural selection. The strongest male plants

produce the most pollen, the strongest female plants produce the most seeds, so locally adapted plants quickly emerge.

Hemp soon spread from its original cultivation in south central Asia in both domesticated and wild forms. From Asia, hemp reached the Middle East by 7,000 B.C. Hemp seeds were found in a German archaeological site dating from 5,000 B.C., when it was also present in the Ukraine and southern Russia. All the classic Mediterranean civilizations knew and used hemp. Early Egyptian textiles were predominately flax-derived linen, but hemp was cultivated in Egypt for ropemaking and sailmaking by 3,000 B.C. Hemp was widely grown in Greece, and reached Italy and Sicily by 100 B.C. The Vikings used hemp for their long boat sails and rigging.

The Scythians spread hemp widely in their military campaigns, bringing it to present day Romania in 700 B.C. The early historian Herodot wrote that the Dacians (Romanian ancestors) used the plant to heal wounds and burns, while Dacian women were highly skilled in using hemp to make clothes. Over time, hemp processing became the main activity of rural Romanian women, which sparked many traditional uses. In some Romanian regions, the old traditional ways of growing and processing hemp within the household have remained unchanged to the present day.

The Romans purposefully took hemp into western and northern Europe. Pedanius Dioscorides, a Greek-born physician traveling through the Roman Empire with Emperor Nero's army, collected and cataloged samples of local medicinal herbs from Italy, Greece, northern Africa, Gaul, Persia, Egypt, and Armenia. It was Dioscorides who first referred to hemp as "cannabis," a Latinized derivative of the Greek word "kannabis." Dioscorides' five volume pharmaceutical book, *De Materia Medica*, published around 65 A.D., was a cornerstone of medicinal education for a thousand years. Widespread use of these medical books led in turn to widespread use of the term cannabis. Some etymologists hold that Dioscorides was actually referring to higher psychoactive hemp strains that were new to the Mediterranean region rather than the fiber-producing hemp that had been grown there for thousands of years.

Wind-blown pollen can travel several miles.

Humans and Hemp
{THC Marijuana Emerges in South Asia}

The hemp moving westward from central Asia was grown predominately for its fiber, so strains with long, straight stalks were favored. However, as hemp spread south some strains began to develop higher levels of THC (tetrahydrocannabinol), a psychoactive chemical which acts like the endocannabinoid chemicals naturally occurring in the human body. Endocannabinoids are found throughout the body: in the brain, organs, connective tissues, glands, and immune cells. These chemicals are a critical component of cell regulation - they work to maintain a stable internal cell environment despite fluctuations in the external environment. For example, at the site of a bodily injury cannabinoids stabilize the nerve cell to prevent excessive firing, and calm nearby immune cells to prevent harmful release of pro-inflammatory substances. Cannabinoid receptors are concentrated in areas of the brain associated with thinking, memory, pleasure, coordination and time perception. When THC attaches to these receptors it correspondingly affects all of those brain functions to varying degree.

In south China, and especially in India, growing and using hemp was a very different experience than the fiber-focused cultivation in the original farming areas and in Europe. As hemp cultivation first moved south in China, it began with the traditional uses of making rope, clothing, fishing nets and superior bowstrings. It was an essential resource for economic life. One indicator of its great cultural significance was the practice of wearing hemp-fabric clothes while mourning the death of a parent or parents, a practice established by the *Li Chi* (Book of Rites) in the second century B.C.

As higher THC strains emerged, hemp became an important pharmaceutical herb, used as medicine as early as 3000 B.C. Cannabis was recognized as one of the 50 fundamental herbs of traditional Chinese medicine. According to legend, Emperor Shen Nung included hemp in a book on medical treatments that he wrote in 2737 B.C. The first recognized medical encyclopedia, *Pen Ts'ao Ching*, lists cannabis as a useful drug in treating gout, rheumatism, malaria, beriberi, constipation and many other ailments. In one of the greatest medicinal breakthroughs of all time, during the second century A.D. the Chinese surgeon Hua T'o combined cannabis resin with wine and created the first effective anesthesia.

Hemp, known as "ma" in China, was considered a unique drug because it had both feminine and masculine plants. For the Chinese, the male and female cannabis plants jointly had the yin and yang required for harmony and good health.

Chinese Symbol for "ma" (hemp)

When yin and yang were out of balance, the body was in a state of disequilibrium and susceptible to illness. The female plant produced more medicine, through its seeds and leaf resins, so the Chinese favored the cultivation of female plants. In addition to its medicinal use, hemp played a crucial role in the Chinese invention and perfection of paper, an event of global importance. The first paper, probably produced around 200 B.C., was made of rags, hemp fiber and tree bark.

By 1,000 B.C., hemp had been carried by traders and nomads into India through the network of trade routes that crossed the Himalayas. In India, cannabis became associated with religious ritual, closely associated with one of the principle Hindu gods - Shiva. The Vedas, the oldest scriptures in Hinduism, describe cannabis as one of five sacred plants with a guardian angel living in its leaves. There are multiple mythical linkages between Shiva and hemp. In one version, Shiva wandered off into the fields after a lengthy argument with his family. Exhausted by the drama and the tropical sun, he fell asleep under a leafy plant. Upon awakening, Shiva decided to sample the leaves of the plant that had so pleasantly shaded his sleep. Before the first taste, Shiva was still worn out from his recent ordeal. With the first bite of hemp he was instantly refreshed, so the god responded by making the plant his favorite food. In an alternative version, all the gods vigorously churned an ocean of milk using a giant snake and an entire mountain until they found an elixir of immortality. As they carried their treasure back into the Himalayas, the gods spilled a few drops of the magical water. At each place where a drop was spilled, miracles occurred. Shiva, deathly ill after being poisoned by the snake as the ocean was churned, went to one of these miracle places in the mountains. There he found a cannabis plant, ate it, and was instantly healed.

Taking their cue from Shiva, for 3000 years Hindus have used "bhang," a liquid paste with ground female cannabis leaves as its foundation. The paste is mixed with yogurt or milk, almonds or other nuts,

spices such as cardamom or cinnamon, and rose water to create a milkshake-thick green drink called a bhang lassi. THC is not water soluble, but milk or yogurt contains fat, and mixing cannabis with fat stretches out its cannabinoid receptor effect. The drink is an important component of many festivals, particularly Holi, the Hindu festival of color and spring. Bhang is also rolled into small balls and eaten. Bhang is generally similar in strength to Western marijuana, but Indians also developed stronger THC variants - ganja and charas. Ganja is made from the flowers and upper leaves of the female plant. Charas, the most potent of the three, contains the most psychoactive resin because it is made directly from blooming flowers. Both ganja and charas are communally smoked in an earthenware pipe called a chillum.

Trade opportunities and rivalries brought several European seafaring countries into India beginning in the 15th century. The Portuguese, Dutch, Danes, and French were eventually supplanted by the British. By the middle of the 19th century Great Britain had gained direct or indirect control over India. The British were quite familiar with the fiber-producing hemp grown in England, but were concerned about the widespread

Photo by Nila Newsom/Shutterstock.com

Photo by AJP/Shutterstock.com

"The resin of the cannabis Indica is in general use as an intoxicating agent from the furthermost confines of India to Algiers. If this resin be swallowed, almost invariably the inebriation is of the most cheerful kind, causing the person to sing and dance, to eat food with great relish, and to seek aphrodisiac enjoyment.

The intoxication lasts about three hours, when sleep supervenes; it is ot followed by nausea or sickness, nor by any symptoms, except slight giddiness, worth recording."

— Source: "The Indian Hemp," The Western Journal of Medicine and Surgery, May 1843.

use of psychoactive cannabis in India. Beginning in 1790, the British taxed the consumption of cannabis products. In an unusual move, in 1893 they commissioned a major scientific study - The Indian Hemp Drugs Commission Report. British and Indian medical experts conducted more than 1,455 interviews and produced nearly 4,000 pages of data and conclusions. The central questions were whether or not cannabis use was harmful to the body or if it led to psychoses. The Commission concluded that suppressing the use of herbal cannabis was unwarranted because its use was an established part of the culture, has religious significance for Hindus, and was harmless in moderation.

Most hemp has seven leaf lobes per stem, but there is some variation among different strains.

Humans and Hemp
{Hemp Reshapes the World through the European Age of Discovery}

The Age of Discovery began in the early 15th century and lasted 250 years. Western European countries aggressively explored the world in search of new trading partners, new goods, and new trade routes. Exploration was driven by the need for a better route for the spice and silk trades. Historically three main trade routes connected Asia to Europe 1) the overland Silk Road from China across Central Asia to the Black Sea; 2) by ship to the Persian Gulf, and then overland through Baghdad or Damascus to Mediterranean ports; or 3) by ship up the Red Sea then overland to Alexandria. The emergence and expansion of the Ottoman Empire threatened these routes. When the Ottoman Turks conquered Constantinople in 1453, they blocked European access to the Middle East and the Red Sea, severely restricting trade.

Even before Constantinople fell, the Portuguese actively sought a new route to China. Prince Henry the Navigator commissioned the first voyages in 1420, designed to explore and map the west coast of Africa in preparation for an eventual journey around the Horn. Vasco da Gama led the first Portuguese expedition around Africa to India. His fleet of four vessels set sail on July 7, 1497 and reached India on May 14, 1498. The return trip began on August 29, 1498 and reached Lisbon in September 1499. Of the 168 men who began the voyage, only 44 returned. Despite these losses, the historic voyage was considered a success. The new route to India drastically changed Europe and the course of world history.

Hemp made the Age of Discovery possible. While the first hemp-outfitted explorers went to India, very quickly interest turned toward the west. Christopher Columbus and the Europeans who followed him reached the New World in ships powered by hemp. Were it not for hemp, European exploration and settlement of the Western Hemisphere would certainly not have occurred as they did. The most popular fabric for sails from the earliest times through the mid-nineteenth century was linen made from flax, but a more coarsely woven hemp fabric was also widely used. Nearly all of the ropes and rigging on sailing vessels were made of hemp because it had a natural resistance to rot, mildew, and mold. It also held up well when exposed to saltwater, which made it indispensable for maritime use. As European navies and seafaring efforts expanded, so did the importance of hemp. The maritime expansion created a booming market for fiber-producing hemp. Each sailing ship needed tons of sails, ropes, and riggings. As an example, the forty-four-gun frigate the U.S.S. Constitution (Old Ironsides) needed two full sets of sails, each set amounting to about three-quarters of an acre of fabric. Fully rigged, she carried 100 tons of hemp rope and riggings. All this material had to be replaced every two to three years. Finally, ships were caulked and made watertight with a hemp-based tarred oakum. Hemp was so crucial to sailing

Outfitting the USS Constitution required 100 tons of hemp.

that ships carried hemp seed to sow in new lands, an insurance policy for a future time when a damaged ship might need to refit sails and ropes for the homeward journey.

The English monarchy recognized that hemp was an essential resource for the navy. In 1533, King Henry VIII issued a royal decree ordering each farmer to set aside a quarter acre of land for hemp for each sixty acres farmed. Failure to comply would result in a fine. Thirty years later Queen Elizabeth I reinforced this decree, and increased the fine for noncompliance. Royal decrees notwithstanding, arable land in England was limited, and domestic production of hemp fell far short of the Royal Navy's needs. The British attempted to quickly develop a hemp industry in the new American colonies, but progress was slow. Out of sheer necessity, England began to import increasing amounts of hemp from Russia, which was the dominate global hemp producer at that time. At the end of the 18th century, Russia grew 80 percent of the world's hemp, with the yearly crop accounting for 20 percent of the value of all Russian exports. The growing British dependence upon Russian hemp was a key component in the frictions which eventually led to the lengthy period of 19th century warfare that reshaped Europe.

Henry VIII tried to increase English hemp production.
Photo by Sergey Goryachev/Shutterstock.com

Humans and Hemp
{Europe Goes to War over Hemp}

By the end of the 18th century, Europe's Age of Discovery had ended, replaced by a string of conflicts over territory and trade. Fighting was expensive, and the least capable of the monarchies soon found themselves in economic and political trouble. The French nobility, with the wild excesses of the Court at Versailles, were the first to fall. The remaining European nobility were understandably nervous about the new government that arose after the first phase of the French Revolution (1789 - 1793). The French army, under the leadership of Napoleon Bonaparte, was proving to be a formidable foe. The nobility feared a continent-wide revolution of commoners - a fear that was quite reasonable following the execution of King Louis XVI and his wife Marie Antoinette in 1793.

In 1793, Britain used its substantial naval advantage over the French (661 vessels to 291) to successfully blockade France and its allies on the Continent. Further, Britain absolutely controlled access to and from the Mediterranean by virtue of its fortifications on the Strait of Gibraltar. Napoleon realized that he could never directly defeat the English navy, so he tried to use his powerful land army, and economics, to weaken the enemy by denying access to Russian hemp.

After defeating a Russian army in 1807, Napoleon forced Czar Alexander to sign the Treaty of Tilsit. The treaty forbade all Russian trade with Great Britain, its allies, or any other neutral nation ship acting as an agent for Great Britain. Napoleon knew that stopping Russian hemp would fatally cripple Britain's navy over time.

Out of necessity and desperation, the English developed a remarkable response to the Treaty of Tilsit. The British boarded American ships in the Atlantic, and brought them to English ports. There, the Americans were offered a secret deal - they could lose their ship and cargo or they could go buy Russian hemp with British gold. The Americans would benefit in two ways, the British would pay them more gold upon their return to England and they were allowed to trade their original cargo to Russia for even more hemp to sell to the British. Not surprising, most American captains and crews opted for the safety and profitability of secretly working with the British.

As European hostilities increased after the French Revolution, American shippers took advantage of the situation by carrying much of the trade between Europe and the French and Spanish islands in the West Indies. As long as shippers broke the passage with a stop in a U.S. port, they evaded seizure under the British rule of 1756. However, in 1806, a British court ruled that U.S. ships breaking passage at an American port had no general protection. The seizure of American ships by Great Britain increased.

Napoleon invaded Russia to stop the flow of hemp to England.

> **"** Britain's crucial need for naval stores and Russia's sybaritic need for gold would always bring them together despite all political differences, like lust drawing together two sensualists despite disparate backgrounds and mutual dislike. **"**
>
> — Alfred W. Crosby, Jr.
>
> — Source: America, Russia, Hemp, and Napoleon (1965) pg. 37

This presented a real problem for the Americans. The combination of Great Britain's blockade of the European coast and Napoleon's Continental System, intended to exclude British goods from countries under French control, threatened the American merchant fleet with confiscation by one side or the other on every trip. Although the French occasionally boarded American ships, the difficulties with the English were more frequent. When the Royal Navy began to impress sailors alleged to be British from U.S. vessels it sparked a national surge of anti-British feeling. President Jefferson hoped to achieve a peaceful settlement, but was ultimately unsuccessful.

When Napoleon learned of the subterfuge of American ships carrying hemp to England, he insisted that Czar Alexander stop all trade with the Americans since they were being coerced into being illegal traders. Napoleon wanted to station French agents and troops in Kronstadt to ensure the Russian port authorities live up to the treaty. The Czar rejected this proposal, and continued to allow trade with American ships. The Czar had a clear interest in allowing this, he needed the profitable trade goods the Americans were bringing in and he definitely needed the gold from the British underground purchases of hemp.

The hemp-selling Russians watched the deterioration of Anglo-American relations with growing horror. Russia knew that war between Britain and the U. S. would immediately end all Russo-American trade because the U.S. ships could not break the British blockade. This would force a choice between economic catastrophe or war with France. If American ships were blocked the Czar would either have to accept a staggering reduction in commerce or would have to take up direct trade with Britain again. Direct trade with Britain would bring Napoleon's army against Russia.

In 1810, Napoleon ordered the Czar to stop all trade with the American traders, but the Russians responded by withdrawing from the part of the Treaty of Tilsit that restricted selling goods to neutral ships. Napoleon, furious over this betrayal, built up his Grand Army and invaded Russia in 1812 to topple the Czar and stop the hemp trade. In the same year, tensions between the U.S. and Great Britain broke out into the War of 1812.

While the Grand Army defeated the Russians in multiple battles and occupied Moscow, the Czar's government did not collapse. In the military campaign and disastrous retreat from Moscow through the nightmarish Russian winter, the Grand Army suffered 90 percent casualties. The campaign failed to meet its primary goal, Russian hemp still found its way to England and the blockade continued. After the decimation of the Grand Army in the retreat from Moscow, Prussia and Austria broke their allegiance with France. In the resulting War of the Sixth Coalition, the monarchies defeated the French and drove Napoleon into exile.

Humans and Hemp
{Hemp Comes to North America}

Hemp likely reached North America before Europeans, carried from Asia by migratory birds. Several early French and English explorers wrote of seeing large hemp fields, although there is some confusion as to whether or not it was actually cannabis. The presence of native hemp notwithstanding, imported hemp seed was a priority in the new colonies. In 1606, French botanist Louis Hebert planted the first cultivated hemp crop in North America in Port Royal, Acadia. Hemp was one of the first crops that Champlain planted at Port Royal and later at Québec.

Given the navy's essential need for hemp and the demonstrated inability to meet that need with domestic resources, England hoped that its North American colonies could help meet the ever-growing demand. At the establishment of Jamestown in 1607, hemp was a recommended planting. In New Plymouth, a 1639 law required each household to plant a minimum stand of hemp. Connecticut followed with a similar requirement. From 1705 to 1737 the British government tried to jump start the industry by offering a bounty of 6 pound sterling for each ton of American-grown hemp. Virginia, Pennsylvania, and Maryland adopted laws making hemp legal tender to encourage production. However, these incentives were insufficient because hemp required a considerable amount of labor in harvesting and preparation of the stalks. Labor was scarce and expensive in America, and farmers could make higher profits with grain, rice, or tobacco.

In Canada, hemp was grown from the beginning of European settlement. As in the American colonies, hemp cultivation was encouraged and subsidized by government. In 1801, the Lieutenant Governor of Upper Canada distributed hemp seeds to farmers. In 1822, the provincial parliament of Upper Canada allocated money for the purchase of machinery to process hemp and additional funds for repairs. But in Canada, as in the U.S., the labor requirements dampened

Male plants begin to produce pollen in early July.

farmer interest in growing large amounts of hemp.

Even though hemp would grow almost anywhere in the colonies, the North Americans joined the British in importing Russian-produced fiber. Adding insult to injury, the early hemp produced in the colonies tended to be unsuitable for maritime use. This was not a problem of plant genetics, but a result of processing techniques. Colonial hemp was generally "dew-retted" - letting the harvested stalks lay on the ground for three or four weeks so moisture could break down the viscous gum that bound the bast fibers to the core. Russian fiber was produced using "water-retting" - immersing the cut stocks into water for eight weeks. Water-retting produces higher quality fiber, but is much more labor intensive and requires large

Kentucky Congressman Henry Clay was a staunch supporter of hemp.

amounts of clean water. The cleaner the water, the better the fiber, so the Russians moved the hemp multiple times during the retting period. Moving the stalks required the tremendous amount of labor that the colonies simply did not have. Water-retting also presented two substantial environmental concerns - dissolving the gum in water emitted a foul odor and released toxic chemicals that killed fish, and would even kill livestock that drank from the used water. While water-retting created environmental concerns, dew-retting actually returned many of the nutrients used by the plant back to the soil. Hemp could be planted for multiple years on dew-retted plots with only a gradual loss of production.

After gaining independence from Great Britain, increasing domestic hemp drew the attention of the new national government. Thomas Jefferson wrote, "Hemp is of first necessity to the wealth and protection of the country." The Tariff Act of 1789 put a tariff on imported hemp to increase the demand for and profitability of domestic production. The Tariff Act of 1828, championed by Kentucky hemp farmer Henry Clay, increased the tax on hemp to sixty dollars a ton, but the U.S. still relied on Russian imports. For example, in 1839 the ropewalk in Charlestown, Mass., used 2,733 tons of hemp to produce rope and rigging for the navy. Of the total, 2,500 tons were Russian hemp, 200 tons were Manila hemp, and 33 tons were American hemp. A "ropewalk" was a long covered

walk or low building with stations for manufacturing long, large diameter rope. To construct a rope, workers attached a strand of hemp fiber to a hand-turned twisting loop, then walked backward feeding the fiber through the loop. As the worker neared the end of one fiber strand, another worker added a new strand and the process continued.

Over time, U.S. hemp production moved west. Kentucky became the hub of the hemp industry after the first plantings near Danville in 1775. Most of Kentucky's hemp was grown in the "Bluegrass" region in the northern part of the state. In 1811, there were at least 50 ropewalks in the state, and by the late 1850s, more than one-third of the 400 bagging, bale rope and cordage factories in America were located there. Between the 1770s through late 1850s, 160 Kentucky factories manufactured hemp products including rope, cloth and floor covering. Slave labor was often used in both the growing and processing of hemp. The growth of cotton growing had a strong positive impact on hemp because dew-retted cordage was well-suited to make the twine used to tie up cotton bales for shipping. Southern cotton growers became the chief market for Kentucky hemp.

Production and prices fluctuated yearly, but the overall trend was toward greater profitability until the 1850s.

Kentucky hemp growers had strong allies in Congress, who tried to increase the use of domestic fiber by the U.S. Navy through various incentive systems. For example, in the 1840s Secretary of Navy George Bancroft sought to give the Kentuckians a competitive advantage by establishing a naval inspection station near the growing areas. This would effectively shift the cost of transportation of the manufactured cordage from the growers to the navy. Kentucky growers developed a locally-adapted strain of hemp from a combination of both Chinese and European lineages. The Kentucky hemp was tall, with quick maturation. Fields commonly yielded five to eight tons of dry

Hemp harvesting was labor intensive.

stalks per acre. Production reached a peak in 1850, followed by several years of bad weather and poor yields. As often happens in agricultural markets, as production faltered prices rose, reaching $180 per ton in 1856. The years of poor harvests convinced many hemp growers to convert to other crops. On the eve of the Civil War, hemp production was moving west again, with Missouri seeing increased production.

The onset of the Civil War dealt domestic hemp production a severe blow. Growers in Missouri and Kentucky were prohibited from selling baling twine to the cotton-producing states that seceded in 1861. Market prices quickly fell by 50 percent or more, and most of the ropewalk facilities were soon shuttered. The explosive expansion of the navy during the war sparked a rapid adoption of new technologies that bypassed hemp.

Ships powered by sail were replaced by steamships, and much of the rigging was now made of twisted wire. New imported fibers like jute from the Philippines replaced hemp in maritime ropes. Burley tobacco became more profitable than hemp as a cash crop in the Bluegrass region. The fall in hemp production was staggering - from nearly 150 million pounds of fiber in 1859 to only 12 million pounds in 1899. In 1899 the Census of Agriculture identified only 964 hemp farmers in the entire country. The average value of the crop that year was 4.6 cents per pound or $34 per acre.

The beginnings of mechanized agriculture with the introduction of the McCormick mechanical reaper seemed to hold the promise for a market rebound because the new wheat production technology used vast amounts of twine. The cut wheat was tied into sheaves

with twine and stacked in shocks to dry before threshing. Twine manufacturers experimented with hemp in the 1880s and 1890s to determine its tensile strength and knotting qualities, and found it "sufficiently tenacious for all the purposes of binding twine." Unfortunately for hemp growers, lower-cost henequen and sisal fibers imported from Mexico also made quality twine.

Hemp production continued its decline. In 1929, there were only 122 farms in the entire U.S. growing hemp. Total production fell to 1.2 million pounds. Once dominant Kentucky only had 5 hemp farmers in 1929, producing 217,000 pounds of fiber. Wisconsin was now the production hub, with 113 producers growing 820,000 pounds of fiber. The Wisconsin results did spill over into an interest in hemp in neighboring states. Minnesota, North Dakota and South Dakota initiated experimental production. Glowing reports stressed the suitability of soil and climatic conditions of the region. The value of hemp as a farm product was emphasized, but the booster reports made no mention of the fact that from 1880 to 1933 the hemp grown in the United States had declined from 15,000 to 1,200 acres, and that the price of hemp cordage had dropped from $12.50 per pound in 1914 to $9.00 per pound in 1933.

The final nail in hemp's coffin came with passage of the 1937 Marijuana Tax Act. This law required that any person who produced marijuana (which was defined as the leaves and flowers of the cannabis plant) had to pay a tax for a stamp to legally cultivate the plant. Since the hemp stalk needs leaves to grow, fiber-producing farmers were also required to pay the tax for the stamp.

Interestingly, the tax act came at a time the hemp industry had some hope for a rebound. New processing machinery developed in Europe, like the "Decorticator," dramatically reduced fiber production costs. The decorticator separated the long hemp fibers from the pulpy celluloid center of the hemp stalks without retting. This reduced the labor time and costs associated with the traditional methods of cleaning and preparing hemp for further processing.

In 1938, *Popular Mechanics* magazine featured hemp in its cover article, declaring it the "new billion dollar crop," but by then it was too late.

Hemp grown for fiber can reach 18 feet tall.

Unfortunately, the Kentucky strain is now considered extinct because the seed stock held at the USDA's National Seed Storage Laboratory was discarded in the 1950s because hemp was no longer considered an important fiber resource.

Humans and Hemp
{Hemp For Victory Program}

World War II brought a brief period of renewed interest in hemp because the Indian, East Asian and Philippine sources of rough fibers like jute were controlled by the Japanese. In 1942, the Department of Agriculture launched a campaign to increase U.S. hemp production to compensate for the loss of other materials. A famous propaganda film, "Hemp for Victory," was produced and released as a newsreel feature. The 14 minute film described the long relationship between humans and hemp, and featured the importance of hemp to the navy. In a famous quip, the narrator says: "For the sailor, no less than the hangman, hemp was indispensable." In 1942, farmers planted 36,000 acres of hemp at the government's request. The patriotic producers still had to have the tax stamp. Cultivation jumped, with more than 100 million pounds of fiber produced annually in 1943 and 1944. At the end of the war, the federal government then reapplied the brakes, and cultivation fell to only a few experimental sites in Wisconsin, with all production ending by 1958.

The demise of active cultivation was certainly not the end of hemp in the United States. The adaptability of the plant gave it the ability to self-procreate. Across the Midwest and Great Plains, "landrace" strains of hemp continue to

thrive. A landrace is defined as a wild growing cannabis strain that evolved in a specific geographic region. In a first-class illustration of Darwinian evolution, over time these wild strains take on their own distinct traits best suited for survival in the region in which they grow. Landrace strains, often known as "ditchweed" are easily found along fence lines, railroad tracks, and stream banks all across the central U.S. Ditchweed grows best in areas with fertile soil and annual rainfall of at least 20 inches.

At the end of World War II the hemp industry in Kentucky appeared to have vanished. In times of stress, however, when fiber is needed and prices are high, it may appear again. Once more perhaps the distinctive odor of growing hemp will hang heavily in the summer air, and the fields of emerald green may once again add beauty to the Kentucky landscape.

— Source: James F. Hopkins (1951) A History of the Hemp Industry in Kentucky

By early June, landrace hemp is well established in South Central Nebraska.

Humans and Hemp
{Hemp Becomes Tangled with Marijuana and Opioids}

While the latter part of the 19th century, with the development of steamships and the emergence of rope alternatives like imported jute, presented real challenges to profitable hemp cultivation, the first half of the 20th century was catastrophic. Hemp became legally tangled with opioids and marijuana, the psychoactive variant of cannabis, and its domestic cultivation was effectively criminalized and eliminated.

The early years of the 20th century brought great changes to the U.S. The increasing urbanization of the population created serious public health issues. As food/drug producers and consumers became geographically and demographically disconnected, it created profitable opportunities for unscrupulous businessmen. Mislabeled, non-nutritious, and even remarkably dangerous ingredients were routinely used as food and drug additives. Eventually, public pressure for reform led to passage of the Federal Food and Drug Act of 1906, one of the first acts of government regulation of market activity.

There was a long national history of aggressive marketing of "patent medicines," over-the-counter trademarked pharmaceuticals. Prior to 1906, ingredients were not listed on labels so consumers were unaware of the actual contents of the remedies. A typical example was "Mrs. Winslow's Soothing Syrup," created by two druggists in 1845 to cure teething pain and other childhood ailments. The product was heavily advertised, with ads featuring idyllic images of mother and child. Because the three primary ingredients in Mrs. Winslow's Soothing Syrup were morphine, alcohol and sugar, it is not surprising that the syrup relieved pain. In an unknown number of cases, the syrup created morphine addiction and even infant death. Documents from a 1868 court case reported that the producers sold more than 1.5 million bottles annually. "Mrs. Winslow's" was labeled a "babykiller" in a special 1912 American Medical Association publication titled *Nostrums and Quackery,* but the potion continued to be sold.

The Food and Drug Act was not aimed at cannabis, but it did require that any potions containing cannabis had to include that on the label. Opioid misuse continued after passage of the Food and Drug Act, so the government responded with the Harrison Narcotics Tax Act of 1914. This gave the federal government

> Winslow's Soothing Syrup, as every physician knows, is one of the morphine-containing "babykillers." Before the federal Food and Drug Act went into effect, no hint of the presence of this dangerous drug was given the purchaser.
>
> **American Medical Association**
>
> — Source: Nostrums and Quackery (1912)

<blockquote>
❝ The first true marijuana scare in the country occurred in El Paso, Texas, on New Year's day 1913, when a Mexican bandito, allegedly crazed by habitual marijuana use, shot up the town and killed a policeman, prompting the city to ban marijuana two years later. ❞

– Dale H. Gieringer

— Source: The Origins of California's 1913 Cannabis Law (2012)
</blockquote>

responsibility to regulate drugs like heroin, opium, morphine, and cocaine, which previously had been sold over-the-counter without restriction. Now, the drugs could only be legally distributed through a prescription written by a licensed medical doctor. The Harrison Act made no direct mention of hemp or cannabis.

The foundational shift in public attitudes toward hemp began when the Mexican Revolution of 1910 pushed a flood of immigrants into the southwestern U.S. Psychoactive cannabis had been introduced into Mexico via the West Indies in the 1800s. Easy and cheap to grow, process and store, the plant spread quickly through Mexico's rural population. Not surprisingly, as that population fled northward during the upheaval of the revolution, the destitute Mexicans carried "marijuana." Thus, the ingestion of cannabis was immediately associated with the newcomers, who were decidedly unwelcome by many U.S. citizens of the time. Anti-drug campaigners warned of the exploding "Marijuana Menace," and horror stories abounded of the terrible crimes attributed to marijuana and its Mexican users.

The ten-year Mexican Revolution pushed thousands of Mexicans into the U.S.

The Mexican Revolution Brings Marjuana to the Southwest

THC containg marijuana plants are shorter than hemp plants, and have more dense foliage.

a prohibition on all recreational drug use. Alcohol prohibition arrived in 1920 after ratification of the 18th Amendment.

Massachusetts was the first state to restrict marijuana, banning it in 1911. California lawmakers attached an obscure clause to that state's 1913 Poison Act Amendments which outlawed the possession of "extracts, tinctures, or other narcotic preparations of hemp, or locoweed, their preparations or compounds (except corn remedies containing not more than fifteen grains of the extract or fluid extract of hemp to the ounce, mixed with not less than five times its weight of salicylic acid combined with collodion)." Other governments soon followed California in banning cannabis: Maine, Wyoming and Indiana in 1913; New York City in 1914; Utah and Vermont in 1915; Colorado and Nevada in 1917. By 1931, 29 states had outlawed marijuana.

The initial regulatory response from the federal government was to encourage individual states to deal with the marijuana issue. The Federal Bureau of Narcotics (FBN) was created in 1930, with Harry J. Anslinger appointed as the first Commissioner of the FBN. He held the position for thirty-two years. Anslinger was a rigid, autocratic leader with a

As marijuana was arriving, the U. S. was also dealing with the issue of alcohol prohibition. After slowly percolating for many years under the banner of the Anti-Saloon League and the Women's Christian Temperance Union, the attack on liquor production and consumption increased around 1910. Prominent businessmen and factory owners often supported prohibition in the hope that banning alcohol would increase the efficiency of their workers and reduce absenteeism and costly accidents. The anti-alcohol arguments were easily stretched to include

background as a private security agent for railroads. At first, Anslinger was relatively unconcerned about cannabis and turned most FBN attention to the international trade in heroin and morphine. When field agents were first making arrests for marijuana possession, Anslinger would chastise them and tell them to "get back to the hard stuff."

Rather than promoting federal legislation specifically aimed at cannabis, the FBN strongly encouraged state governments to accept responsibility for control of the problem by adopting the Uniform State Narcotic Act. This Act encouraged states to pass state laws matching the federal Narcotic Drug Import and Export Act of 1922. Cannabis use was thought of as a regional problem in the southwest, so no nationwide response was warranted. However,

Anslinger soon decided that attacking marijuana would build public and political support for his agency. With the director's blessing the FBN used movies and newspapers to mount a fullout propaganda assault on cannabis in the mid-1930s. Although most Americans did not even know what marijuana looked like, sensationalist media stories began to stoke public concern. Marijuana users were depicted as sex-crazed, violently psychotic savages who were impervious to pain and reason. Movies like *Refeer Madness (1936), Marihuana, The Devil's Weed (1936) and Assassin of Youth (1937)* reinforced the FBN message that one puff of marijuana was a life-altering experience. Cleancut teenagers transformed into promiscuous, homicidal maniacs while under the influence.

According to Hollywood, these teens were at extreme risk from marijuana

" The motion picture you are about to witness may startle you. It would not have been possible, otherwise, to sufficiently emphasize the frightful toll of the new drug menace which is destroying the youth of America in alarmingly increasing numbers. Marihuana is that drug a violent narcotic an unspeakable scourge The Real Public Enemy Number One! "

— Opening Scene
Reefer Madness (1936)

The term "marihuana" means all parts of the plant Cannabis sativa L., whether growing or not; the seeds thereof; the resin extracted from any part of such plant; and every compound, manufacture, salt, derivative, mixture, or preparation of such plant, its seeds or resin. Such term does not include the mature stalks of such plant, fiber produced from such stalks, oil or cake made from the seeds of such plant, any other compound, manufacture, salt, derivative, mixture, or preparation of such mature stalks (except the resin extracted therefrom), fiber, oil, or cake, or the sterilized seed of such plant which is incapable of germination.

– Controlled Substances Act
of 1970

A low point for hemp came when Rep. Robert L. Houghton of North Carolina introduced the Marijuana Tax Act in Congress on April 14, 1937. The Act made no distinction between psychoactive marijuana and fiber-producing hemp and was designed to eliminate the production of cannabis through a prohibitive tax requirement. Commissioner Anslinger came up with the Act, which restricted possession of cannabis to individuals who paid an excise tax. However, the Act created an impossible Catch 22 - to comply with the law by paying the tax, an American would have to effectively admit that he/she were in illegal possession of cannabis. Congress held two hearings to debate the Act, with a total of one hour of testimony and discussion. When the American Medical Association (AMA)

Legislative Counsel suggested that the available evidence did not support the current media portrayal, the Committee responded by telling the witness he should refrain from "trying to throw obstacles in the way of something that the federal government is trying to do." The AMA opposed the bill because it would force physicians who prescribed cannabis to buy the marijuana stamp. Debate in the House lasted 90 seconds, just long enough for a committee member to falsely report that the AMA gave the bill its full support. The outcome in the Senate was similar - one brief hearing and overwhelming approval. Canada followed the U.S. lead in 1938 with passage of the Opium and Narcotics Control Act.

In 1969 the Supreme Court ruled the Marijuana Tax Act unconstitutional because it violated the Fifth Amendment protection against self-incrimination. When Timothy Leary, psychologist, writer, and psychedelic drug activist, was arrested for possession of marijuana he challenged the law on the grounds that the act required self-incrimination, thus violating the Fifth Amendment. The unanimous opinion of the court, written by Justice John Marshall Harlan II, agreed with the challenge and the Marihuana Tax Act was ruled unconstitutional.

While Leary's conviction was overturned, it was not a victory for industrial hemp. Congress responded to the Supreme Court decision by repealing the Marihuana Tax Act and passing the Controlled Substances Act of 1970 to continue the prohibition of cannabis products.

Hemp fared even worse under the Controlled Substances Act than it had under the earlier law. Once again, there was no distinction between hemp and marijuana. All cannabis was listed as a Schedule 1 (most dangerous) drug along with substances like heroin and LSD. Schedule I drugs are those with a high potential for abuse, have no recognized medical use, and are dangerous even when used under medical supervision. Listing all cannabis as a Schedule I drug made it almost impossible for researchers to study any strain of the plant. Researchers had to have a full security facility meeting a host of specific requirements for safes, vaults, perimeter fencing, employee monitoring and other measures. Further, potential researchers had to register with the Drug Enforcement Administration (DEA), had to keep accurate and complete records of all transactions involving controlled substances, had to maintain detailed inventories of the substances in their possession, had to periodically file reports with the DEA and accept on-site inspections.

Prohibitions notwithstanding, the 1970s saw a dramatic increase in marijuana use. As more and more people were arrested for possession, there was a growing concern that the penalties were inappropriately harsh. The bipartisan Shafer Commission, appointed by President Nixon at the direction of Congress in 1972, reviewed the laws and medical evidence regarding marijuana and determined that personal use of marijuana should be decriminalized. Nixon rejected the recommendation, but during the 1970s eleven states decriminalized marijuana possession and most others reduced the penalties.

Powerful political forces were unhappy with the easing of marijuana penalties, which prompted passage of the 1986 Anti-Drug Abuse Act. A key feature of the act, signed by President Reagan, was mandatory sentences for drug-related crimes. The new law raised federal penalties for marijuana possession and dealing, basing the penalties on the amount of the drug involved. For example, possession of 100 marijuana plants received the same penalty as possession of 100 grams of heroin. A later amendment to the Anti-Drug Abuse Act established the "three strikes and you're out" policy, requiring life sentences for repeat drug offenders. Finally, seeking the ultimate deterrence, the legislation authorized the death penalty for "drug kingpins."

Hemp Begins Its Return to North America

While many countries followed the U.S. example and banned all cannabis production, cultivation did continue in scattered pockets around the globe. The Chinese, Japanese, Ukrainians, Russians, Hungarians, and French maintained some production. However, even in these countries increased cultivation of cotton and the emergence of synthetic fibers in the 1960s dramatically eroded acreage devoted to hemp. For example, hemp cultivation in the Ukraine fell from 240,000 acres in 1960 to 15,000 in 1993.

In 1994, Canada issued limited licenses to grow hemp for research purposes. This was followed in 1998 with legalization of commercial cultivation, under licenses and authorization issued by Health Canada. The license to grow hemp for grain or fiber was issued for one calendar year for crops on 10 acres or more, or if cultivating for seed, not less than 2.47 acres. Health Canada regulations control the importation, production, processing, possession, sale, transportation, delivery and sale. Canada adopted a 0.3 percent THC standard in the leaves and flowering parts as the legal distinction between hemp and marijuana. As with many new crops, in the early years there was considerable volatility in production acreage. Hemp acreage has increased steadily since 2008, with over 84,000 acres licensed for cultivation in 2015.

Even after hemp cultivation was started in Canada, in the U.S there was still no recognized legal difference between hemp and marijuana. A routine traffic stop in Anchorage, Alaska in 1972 set off a chain of events that ultimately led to a fundamental change in the status of all cannabis. Irwin Ravin, an attorney, was arrested for marijuana possession after being stopped for a broken taillight. He appealed his conviction all the way to the Alaskan Supreme Court, where he based his defense upon his fundamental right to privacy. In 1975, the court ruled in Ravin's favor, effectively allowing cannabis in Alaska for in-home personal use. This decision opened the door for the next major change in the status of cannabis California's legalization of medical marijuana in 1996. Voters passed Proposition 215 by a substantial margin, allowing the medical use of marijuana for patients with AIDS, cancer, and other serious and painful diseases. Alaska, Oregon and Washington followed with similar legislation in 1998. By 2015, 23 states and the District of Columbia had enacted laws legalizing medical marijuana.

Colorado and Washington passed state referendums on November 6, 2012

allowing controlled recreational use of marijuana. Alaska and Oregon followed with a majority of voters approving recreational use in the November 2014 election. At the time, all of these state laws stood in tension with existing federal laws prohibiting possession of marijuana. In the years since passage of Proposition 215, the U.S. Supreme Court had decided two medical marijuana cases affirming federal authority to enforce prohibition laws against patients and providers even when they were in compliance with state laws. The threat of federal action against medical users was quietly ended with a provision in the 2014 budget bill which prohibits federal agents from raiding retail operations in states with legal medical marijuana.

In 2013, the 113th Congress made significant changes to U.S. policies regarding industrial hemp during the omnibus farm bill debate. Section 7606 of the Agricultural Act of 2014, *Legitimacy of Industrial Hemp Research*, defines industrial hemp as distinct from marijuana and authorizes institutions of higher education or a state department of agriculture to conduct research and develop pilot programs if allowed by state laws where the institution is located. The farm bill also established a statutory definition of "industrial hemp" as the plant *Cannabis sativa L.* and any part of such plant with a delta9 tetrahydrocannabinol (THC) concentration of not more than 0.3% on a dry weight basis. On February 7, 2014, President Obama signed the Farm Bill of 2014 into law. Individual states must authorize action before hemp research can begin. As of 2015, 27 states including Nebraska have enacted the authorizing legislation. The Unicameral passed LB 1001 by a vote of 39 - 2, and it was signed by the governor on April 2, 2014. The Legislature stopped short of full hemp legalization, as the measure only makes hemp cultivation legal for research purposes.

The enacted 2015 budget appropriations blocked federal law enforcement authorities from interfering with state agencies, hemp growers, and agricultural research in states with enabling legislation. In 2015, six states had active research crop production underway and three states (Colorado, Oregon, and Vermont) had licensed farmers to cultivate commercial hemp. In June 2015, the Maine legislature overrode the governor's veto of legislation allowing commercial hemp, so Maine producers will be able to grow hemp in 2016.

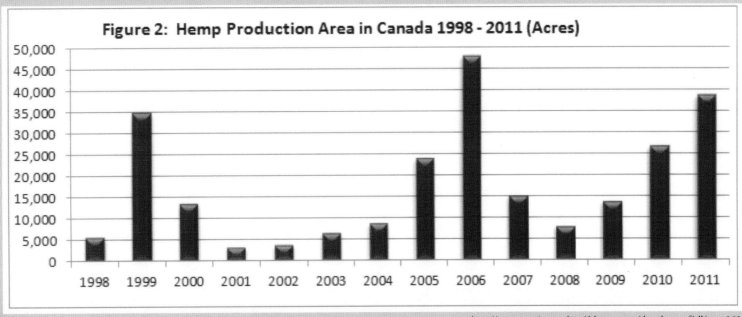

Figure 2: Hemp Production Area in Canada 1998 - 2011 (Acres)

http://www1.agric.gov.ab.ca/$department/deptdocs.nsf/all/econ9631

Humans and Hemp
{Agricultural Groups Support Hemp Production}

The National Farmers Union (NFU) updated its 2013 farm policy regarding hemp to urge the President, Attorney General, and Congress to "direct the U.S. Drug Enforcement Administration (DEA) to reclassify industrial hemp as a non-controlled substance and adopt a policy to allow American farmers to grow industrial hemp under state law without affecting eligibility for USDA benefits." Previously NFU's policy advocated that the DEA "differentiate between industrial hemp and marijuana and adopt policy to allow American farmers to grow industrial hemp under state law without requiring DEA licenses."

The National Association of State Departments of Agriculture (NASDA) "supports revisions to the federal rules and regulations authorizing commercial production of industrial hemp," and has urged USDA, DEA, and the Office of National Drug Control Policy to "collaboratively develop and adopt an official definition of industrial hemp that comports with definitions currently used by countries producing hemp." NASDA also "urges Congress to statutorily distinguish between industrial hemp and marijuana and to direct the DEA to revise its policies to allow USDA to establish a regulatory program that allows the development of domestic industrial hemp production by American farmers and manufacturers."

In 2014, the American Farm Bureau Federation endorsed a policy to support the "production, processing, commercialization, and utilization of industrial hemp," and passed a policy resolution to oppose the "classification of industrial hemp as a controlled substance." Previously, in 1995, the Farm Bureau had passed a resolution supporting "research into the viability and economic potential of industrial hemp production in the United States... [and] further recommend that such research includes planting test plots in the United States using modern agricultural techniques."

The National Grange voted in 2009 to support "research, production, processing and marketing of industrial hemp as a viable agricultural activity."

Regional farmers' organizations also have policies regarding hemp. For example, the North Dakota Farmers Union (NDFU), as part of its federal agricultural policy recommendations, has urged "Congress to legalize the production of industrial hemp." The Rocky Mountain Farmers Union (RMFU) has urged "Congress and the USDA to recommit and fully fund research into alternative crops and uses for crops" including industrial hemp; also, they "support the decoupling of industrial hemp from the definition of marijuana" under the Controlled Substances Act.

Colorado State University hemp research plot, 2016

Humans and Hemp
{Domestic Production Actually Begins in 2013}

In October 2013, Colorado farmer Ryan Loflin made history by harvesting the first commercial domestic hemp crop in 56 years. Loflin had decided to plant 60 acres of hemp on his family's 1200 acre family farm near Springfield, in the southeastern corner of the state, even before the Colorado Department of Agriculture had established rules and regulations for the crop. Using seed imported from Europe, Loflin hand-sowed the crop in June. Seed germination rate was low, and the field was overrun by invasive foxtail, which made mechanical harvesting impossible. Eighty hemp enthusiasts from five states converged on the farm in October to harvest the crop by hand. The first crop was used for multiple purposes, with some of the seeds pressed for oil and stalks and roots used for fiber.

With active cultivation in Colorado, Kentucky, Tennessee, Oregon, and Vermont, U.S. domestic hemp production has now begun. From Loflin's 60 acres in 2013, American farmers grew approximately 250 acres of hemp in 2014. In 2015, domestic acres increased to 5,000-6,000 acres. Market demand for hemp goods has also increased, with retail sales increasing 20 percent from 2013-2014. Hemp derived products now represent a $400 million U.S. market, with 20 percent to 30 percent annual growth through 2020. (2014 retail hemp sales, source: www.HempBizJournal.com)

The beginnings of active cultivation and recent legislative actions have sparked a considerable interest in hemp research, particularly with regard to the medicinal possibilities of CBD.

Suggested Readings:

E. J. W. Barber, Prehistoric Textiles: *The Development of Cloth in the Neolithic and Bronze Ages* (Princeton University Press, 1991).

Peter Bellwood, *First Farmers: The Origin of Agricultural Societies* (Blackwell Publishing, 2005).

Alfred Crosby, *America, Russia, Hemp, and Napoleon* (Ohio State University Press, 1965)

Richard Davenport Hines, *The Pursuit of Oblivion: A Global History of Narcotics* (Weidenfeld & Nicolson, 2012)

James Hopkins, *A History of the Hemp Industry in Kentucky* (University of Kentucky Press, 1951)

Daniel Zohary, Maria Hopf, and Ehud Weis, *Domestication of Plants in the Old World*, Fourth Edition (Oxford University Press, 2012).

Deck of the Cutty Sark, now moored in Greenwich.

Miles and Miles of Hemp Rigging

Larry Carstenson, JD
Model ship Builder for Fifty-five Years

Few sights in nature can match the beauty and majesty of a three-mast clipper ship slicing through the waves under full sail. The clippers, built in the second half of the 19th century, were the apex of the Age of Sail. They were built with economics and speed in mind - the first batch of the new tea harvest from China each year was highly coveted in Victorian England. The first tea to arrive commanded the highest price, and brought national fame to ship and captain. The annual race captured the imagination of the entire populace, with the clippers' progress reported by telegraph and covered in the papers. Fortunes changed hands as huge bets were made on which ship would be the first to dock.

Built for speed, these beautiful ships inspired some of the greatest maritime art of all time, like Montague Dawson's dynamic paintings of the great clippers surging through choppy seas. Or John Robert Spurling's watercolor immortalizing the great tea race of 1872 between the *Cutty Sark* and the *Thermopylae*. Standing before his canvas pulls the viewer back in time. Both ships running with the wind, with acres of deployed sail. One can imagine the sleek black-hulled *Cutty Sark* pulling

ahead of the green-hulled Thermopylae and increasing her lead…pulling ahead by an incredible 400 nautical miles before disaster strikes when a storm off Sumatra tears away her rudder. Imagine the frustration of the captain and crew during the thirteen day repair, knowing that Thermopylae is now the ship pulling further and further away. Imagine oneself standing on deck as the repaired *Cutty Sark* begins the long chase - feel the surge as the sails catch the wind, the ship beneath you racing across the ocean at more than 20 miles per hour. Powered by nothing but the wind through her sails. The sound and power of the wind, the crash of the waves, the sting of the salt spray in one's eyes, a sensory overload that sends chills down the spine of even the most landlocked land lubber. The faster *Cutty Sark* always gaining on the *Thermopylae*, but ultimately unable to overcome the broken rudder in the race home.

This book is about hemp. So, what do the *Cutty Sark* and other sailing ships have to do with hemp? In a word: rope (or "lines," in the words of the true sailor as explained by C. Nepean Longridge in his interesting book *The Anatomy of Nelson's Ships*, Naval Institute Press, 1989.) Without rope, which was exclusively

made of hemp until the 1880s when steel wire came into use, those beautiful sailing ships, and military ships of the line, too, were nothing more than piles of lumber, languishing at an oceanside dock. Hemp was essential to the movement of any ship under sail.

While the great sailing ships no longer have commercial or military importance, we remain fascinated by their elegance.

Model of USS Constitution

There are thousands of model ship builders, and I am one. I built my first model, *The Thermopylae*, in 1960. I have pampered and protected it through countless moves, and am proud to say it is still in excellent condition. Modelers have a variety of kit types - some are plastic, some are wood. I have tried them all. My pride and joy is a wood, plank on frame, replica of the *U.S.S. Rattlesnake*. My plastic model of the U.S.S. Constitution (Old Ironsides) required more than a quarter mile of thread for its rigging, taking hundreds of hours to complete. When it was deployed, the real

Model of USS Rattlesnake

Constitution required 100 tons of hemp. My current project is a very exact wooden replica of Lord Nelson's *H.M.S. Victory*.

It is interesting to note the relative size and complexity of these ships and to see how dependent each was on rope and sails made from hemp. Even the *Rattlesnake*, less than half the size of the *Victory*, took an extraordinary amount of hemp to set sail. Following is a brief description of several selected ships with an explanation of the size, dimensions, crew, lines and sails. These remarkable ships still capture our imagination today.

H.M.S. VICTORY: (Oldest Commissioned warship in the world):

Launch date: 1765
Length: 227.5 feet
Beam width: 51feet, 10 inches
Depth: 28 feet, 9 inches
gross tonnage : 2142
Sail: 174,240 square feet (37 sails, plus 23 sails in reserve)
Complement: 850
Rigging: 137,280 feet of running rigging (largest rope was 19 inches in circumference)
Maximum speed: 10 mph
Guns: 104 (A shot from a 32 pounder guns could penetrate 2 feet thick oak from around 1 mile away.)
Hull was over two feet thick. (Took 5,000 mature oak trees, aged for 14 years after harvest.)

U.S.S. CONSTITUTION

Launch date: 1797
Length: 304 feet
Beam width: 43.5 feet
Depth: 23 feet
gross tonnage : 1576
Complement: 450
Sail: 42710 square feet
Rigging: 42240 feet of running rigging
Maximum speed: 15 mph
Guns: 44 guns (often carrying over 50)

CUTTY SARK:

Launch date: 1869
Length: 212.5 feet
Beam width: 36 feet
Depth: 21 feet
gross tonnage : 963
Complement: 2835
Sail: 32,000 square feet
Rigging: 37,000 feet of running rigging
Maximum speed: 20.1 mph
Guns: None

Partially from: Royce's Sailing Illustrated, Royce Publications, 9th Ed, 1997, Vol. 2, Page 146.

Hemp: The Mexican Connection

Roger Davis, PhD
Professor of History, University of Nebraska at Kearney

Hemp fiber, *cannabis sativa*, known as *cáñamo* in Spanish, arrived in Mexico and Latin America as part of the Columbian exchange beginning in 1492. Hemp fibers comprised the essential ropes, cords and caulking for the world's sailing vessels, as well as providing fiber for sacks, shoes, twine, and other agricultural goods. To meet growing imperial and commercial needs, the Spanish Crown mandated the growing of hemp in Mexico (New Spain) and Chile in 1545 and later expanded that mandate in 1777. While commercial hemp (*cannabis sativa*) was the predominant product, a companion variation of hemp, *cannabis indica*, also emerged in the marketplace. This variant of hemp has pharmaceutical qualities of an intoxicant or hallucinogenic nature. The colonial entrepreneurs knew of this hemp as "marihuana" or "mariguana," (both noted in the Royal Academy Dictionary of the Spanish Language. The common terminology "marijuana" is the Anglicized version of the term.) While commercial hemp became bags and rigging, marihuana, also known as *pipilzintzintlis*, soon joined the array of indigenous potions of peyote, morning glory, coca, and tobacco, used for religious and cultural purposes. Hemp was introduced into California in 1795 as a fiber crop for the missions, but there is no evidence of marihuana cultivation and the hemp production ended with Mexican independence.

A variety of cultivars on a Colorado test plot illustrate hemp's diversity.

As with colonial Mexico, hemp was a commodity of the British colonies, and remained a valued product following independence. The Virginia Assembly in 1619 required farmers to grow hemp and it flourished as well in Pennsylvania, Maryland and later Kentucky. George Washington and Thomas Jefferson invested in hemp cultivation. By the time California joined the nation, following the Treaty of Guadalupe in 1848, domestic hemp was being replaced by imports from Russia, and domestic production of hemp was nearly at an end. With regard to *cannabis indica*, it was known in the United States principally as "hashish," an imported drug from Egypt, Syria, and India, consumed by a bohemian fringe of artists and of intellectuals but of no

particular issue for the general public. Then came the Mexican Revolution and the story of hemp in the United States took a dramatic turn.

The violence and chaos of the Mexican Revolution (1910 - 1920) compelled a significant immigration of Mexican refugees into the United States. It is estimated that over 600,000 Mexicans crossed the border between 1910 and 1930, traversing the southwest from Texas to California. And, in a relatively short period of time there emerged across the United States an awareness of a "marijuana menace" that had to be confronted. It was well known that marijuana use was widespread in Mexico. The English-language newspaper from Mexico City, *The Mexican Herald*, had

been reporting on marijuana use among the military, prisons, indigenous, and poor since the turn of the century. It was well known that revolutionary armies were infested with the drug. This particular variation of hemp was deemed akin to the "loco weed" well known by ranchers to have detrimental effects on cattle and horses. This particular variation of hemp following in the wake of the Mexican migration appeared equally dangerous for humans, causing men to go insane and become unusually violent. In 1913 the *El Paso Herald* reported the killing of a police officer by a Mexican who had become crazed from marijuana use. The following year Los Angeles authorities launched a crackdown on the city's "Sonoratown" as a center of marijuana cultivation, culminating in a public bonfire of a ton of the evil weed.

It became clear that the menace of marijuana required a swift and substantial response. In 1915 El Paso became the first city to enact an ordinance banning the sale or possession of marijuana. In 1930 the newly created Federal Bureau of Narcotics strongly encouraged state government to face the challenge of the drug menace and by 1931 twenty-nine states had outlawed marijuana. In 1936 the classic representation of the danger of marijuana use appeared in the film *Reefer Madness*, and the following year the national government enacted the Marijuana Tax Act, criminalizing the drug and limiting its medical and industrial uses. A brief reprieve for hemp cultivation emerged during World War II as imports of hemp for cordage, parachutes and other necessities were interrupted. The government launched a "Hemp for Victory" program and by 1943 American farmers harvested over 350,000 acres of the fiber. However with the end of the war and the emergence of new synthetic fibers, hemp once again became a one dimensional crop associated primary as a narcotic in need of control and suppression.

Recent scholarship, principally the excellent work of Issac Campos, has shed new light on the topic of the marijuana menace associated with Mexicans and the Mexican immigration. Prior interpretations inferred that the rapid emergence of the drug menace and the legal and bureaucratic mechanisms of suppression were due to the racist culture in the United States and the fear of immigration. Campos convincingly demonstrates that the definition of marijuana as a menace and the need to suppress it is born not in the United States but in Mexico and then imported into the United States on the heels of the immigration experience. From 1870 to 1920, whether the government of Porfirio Diaz, or those of the revolution, Mexican leadership was preoccupied with the image and reality of Mexico and her people. Both Diaz's *cientificos* and leading delegates to the revolutionary constitutional convention of 1917 faced the challenge of the perceived "degeneration" of the nation. Political,

intellectual, and social leaders aspired to "modernity" and desperately wanted Mexico to not only be perceived as modern by other nations but to in fact be a modern people. Consequently, Mexican scholars, scientists, and intellectual leaders identified "degenerate" practices that had to be ended for the good of the nation. Principal among these practices was the use of *mariguana* among the indigenous, poor, criminal, and even military populations. The Mexican Department of Public Sanitation and the Mexican media dramatized the challenge with an outpouring of "scientific" studies and reports of the dangers of mariguana use. The message was uniform across the media, including the Mexican Herald, and in government reports. In March, 1920 the Mexican government defined *mariguana* as an illegal narcotic and banned its production, distribution, and use in a new law entitled, "Dispositions on the Cultivation and Commerce of Products that Degenerate the Race." This impulse and interpretation of the sanctity of the modern, was a dynamic presenting itself across Latin America. Similar scenarios appeared in Brazil, Argentina, Colombia, and Cuba. The array of scientific research which kept a distance from politics and culture concluded that *cannibus indica* was not an extreme narcotic, offered many valuable medicinal qualities, was not a cause of violent or psychotic behavior, and was not the foundation of degeneracy in any community of people. Politically

incorrect, such insights were set aside.

In the United States the modern image of hemp has been viewed through a historical lens which is only now being reconsidered. A crop of our forefathers and one with many positive attributes has suffered from the association with a Mexican mythology of both cultural and scientific distortion.

Suggested Readings:

Isaac Campos, *Degeneration and the Origins of Mexico's War on Drugs, Mexican Studies/Estudios Mexicanos*. V. 26. No 2. Summer, 2010. 379408.

Isaac Campos, *Home Grown: Marijuana and the Origins of Mexico's War on Drugs*. (University of North Carolina Press, 2012).

Dale Gieringer, *The Origins of Cannabis Prohibition in California Contemporary Drug Problems*. (Federal Legal Publication. June, 2006).

Timothy Henderson, *Beyond Borders: A History of Mexican Migration to the United States* (Wiley Blackwell, 2011).

Eric Schlosser, *Reefer Madness*. The Atlantic. August, 1994. 1 – 33.

Matt Thompson, *The Mysterious History of Marijuana*, NPR Code Switch. July 22, 2013. Online

Nebraska's Hemp History

Ronald L. Wirt, PhD
Associate Professor and Coordinator of Library User
Services, University of Nebraska Kearney

According to "Hemp for Victory," when the Japanese Army began its invasion of the Philippines in early December, 1941, it put in danger the primary supplier to the U.S. of a vital strategic resource – Manila hemp fiber, commonly used to make high-quality rope for marine applications such as hawsers (very heavy ship mooring lines), cargo and fishing nets, rope and twine, and other specialty products. By April, 1942, Japanese forces had occupied most of the Philippines. The supply of hemp fiber had been cut off, and U.S. forces were using up their last hemp reserves.

"Hemp for Victory" is a short educational film that was produced by the U.S. Department of Agriculture in 1942. It was intended to motivate American farmers to grow more hemp to support the war effort. According to the film, 36,000 acres had been planted in 1942, with a 1943 goal of 50,000 acres. Following the end of the war, hemp production was abandoned due to provisions of the Marihuana Tax Act of 1937, which outlawed the production of marihuana, and effectively put an end to the cultivation of hemp for industrial, food, and medicinal purposes in the United States. (Robinson 1942, (2016).)

This was not the first effort by the U.S. Government to encourage hemp cultivation in Nebraska, however. A chapter in the *1901 Yearbook of the United States Department of Agriculture* by Lyster Dewey provides a discussion of the hemp plant, optimum soils and growing conditions, industrial uses of hemp fiber (cordage, twine, carpets, linen goods, oakum), and demand, production and import statistics. The report mentions especially the several counties in Kentucky where hemp was grown on a large scale, and notes that hemp has been produced successfully near Havelock (Lancaster County) and Fremont (Dodge County) in Nebraska, as well as near Gridley (Butte County) in California and in the Houston, Texas area. In prior years it was also grown between Champaign and Rantoul, Illinois, and along the Missouri River between St. Joseph and Kansas City, Missouri. Dewey also describes the processes of retting and breaking, both of which are essential to the production of hemp fiber. He notes that about 18,000,000 pounds of hemp was used in the U.S. annually, of which only around 8,500,000 pounds was produced domestically. (Dewey 1902)

As early as 1861, hemp was being

Naturally occurring hemp in Nebraska, late summer

promoted as an ideal alternative to corn and wheat farming in Nebraska. (C.W.G. 1861). Even before government efforts to promote hemp growing, hemp milling and binder twine production was a thriving business in Fremont in 1890, with the mill of Nebraska Hemp and Twine beginning operations in early November of that year. (Nebraska Notes 1890) The company was operating with 40 employees in 1891, (Nebraska State Gazetteer 1890-91), producing over two million pounds "of the best grade of twine, up from 800,000 pounds the previous year. (Walsh 1892). In 1893, it was advertising Victor Hemp Twine in adjoining states, (The Advocate & Topeka Tribune. 1893) and facing competition for both raw materials and retail sales (some would say unfair competition) from the state-owned prison binding twine factory in Stillwater, MN. (Stillwater News 1894) ("The criminals of Minnesota..." 1894). By 1896, it was consuming the raw hemp grown on 2000 acres in the Fremont area, (News and Notes 1896), with a competing facility commencing operations in Havelock in the following year. (Nebraska News Notes 1897). The processing plant in Fremont was destroyed by fire, but was rebuilt in 1899 with a larger production capacity. (Nebraska News Notes 1899). By January, 1900, the rebuilt facility was operating with both day and night shifts, with a total of sixty-five production workers. (Fremont Hemp Mill Opens 1900).

Other government documents have also encouraged the production of hemp, including another USDA Yearbook chapter by R. A. Oakley entitled: "The Seed Supply of the Nation – Hemp," and a USDA Bulletin by Lyster Dewey from 1916 that pointed out that hemp "can produce four times more paper pulp per acre than trees." (Moran 2015), (Dewey & Merrill 1916).

At both the Federal and State levels, there has been interest in permitting research and pilot production on industrial hemp. The 113th Congress made changes to policies during the Omnibus Farm Bill debate, with the final bill allowing limited research. A statutory definition of industrial hemp was also established. The 114th Congress has reintroduced the Industrial Hemp Farming Act of 2015. (Johnson 2015). Brief discussion of the Industrial Hemp Farming Act, sponsored by Senators McConnell, Wyden, Paul, and Merkley, has appeared recently in the Congressional Record. (Wyden 2015). The Nebraska Unicameral passed legislation in 2014 allowing universities to begin growing hemp for research purposes.

References

Dewey, Lyster D, and Jason L Merrill. 1916. Hemp Hurds as PaperMaking Material. Bulletin, U.S. Department of Agriculture, Washington DC: Project Gutenberg. Accessed January 2016. http://www.votehemp.com/17855h/17855h.htm.

Dewey, Lyster. 1902. "The Hemp Industry in the United States." In Yearbook of the United States Department of Agriculture., by U.S. Department of Agriculture. Washington, DC: Government Printing Office. Accessed January 7, 2016. http://babel.hathitrust.org/cgi/pt?id=uc1.b3027217;view=1up;seq=705.

Goad, Frank. 2014. "Can Industrial Hemp Make a Comeback?" The Lane Report, December. Accessed January 11, 2016.

Johnson, Renée. 2015. Hemp as an Agricultural Commodity. Report to Congress, Washington DC: Congressional Research Service, 29 pp. Accessed January 11, 2016.

Moran, Courtney N. 2015. "Industrial Hemp: Canada Exports, United States Imports." Fordham Environmental Law Review (Fordham University). Accessed January 2015.

Robinson, Brittain B. 1942, (2016). "Hemp for Victory (Transcript)." www.hemp.com. Raymond Evans. Accessed January 7, 2016. http://www.hemp.com/historyofhemp/hempforvictory/.

Wyden, Ronald. 2015. National Hemp History Week. United States Senate, Washington DC: Congressional Record, S37623763. Accessed January 6, 2016.

For Further Reading:

2013. "Whole Foods Market Spotlights Hemp Products for Hemp History Week." Food & Beverage CloseUp, 2013.

2014. "Hemp gets its due." Natural Foods Merchandiser 35, no. 5: 11.

Agbor, Valery, Francesco Zurzolo, Warren Blunt, Christopher Dartiailh, Nazim Cicek, Richard Sparling, and David B. Levin. 2014. "Singlestep fermentation of agricultural hemp residues for hydrogen and ethanol production." Biomass and Bioenergy 64, 6269.

Brady, Tara Christine. 2003. "The Argument for the Legalization of Industrial Hemp." San Joaquin Agricultural Law Review 13, 85.

Firger, Jessica.. 2015. "THE UNSMOKABLE GRASS." Newsweek Global 165, no. 15: 50.

Herer, Jack. 1990. "The forgotten history of hemp." Earth Island Journal 5, no. 4: 35.

Richardson, Sarah. 2014. "The smothered history of hemp." American History no. 3: 10.

Thedinger, Seaton. 2006. "Prohibition in the United States: International and U.S. Regulation and Control of Industrial Hemp." Colorado Journal Of International Environmental Law And Policy 17, 419.

Will, Oscar H., III. 2004. "Strategic fibers: the forgotten history of hemp cultivation in America." Farm Collector, 2004. 12.

Note: Renée Johnson lists many other sources of information in her report to the Congress, and notes the list of historical sources at: http://hempology.org/ALLARTICLES.html

Hemp strains exhibit wide color variation

Nebraska's Cannabis Policy

Jackson Osborn

The federal prohibition of all cannabis products in the United States began in 1937 but a multitude of states had already passed laws outlawing possession or cultivation. The Nebraska Unicameral passed a law in the 1927 session that established a state prohibition on cannabis products, with the exception of medicinal use under the control of a physician or pharmacist. The statutes are found in the 1929 *Compiled Statutes of Nebraska*, and are referred to as *State Statutes* 28435 and 28436 respectively. Persons found guilty of importing cannabis faced a fine of $100 to $500 (approximately $1400 to $6800 in current prices) and 1 to 3 years in prison. Penalties were lighter for cultivation, with confinement in the county jail for 3 to 6 months for the first offense and 1 to 2 years in the penitentiary for subsequent convictions.

The original bill was introduced by Lincoln representatives Thomas Axtell and Henry P. Hansen. The bill served as a critical juncture in marijuana policy in the state. When the state legislature was given the task of dealing with marijuana, they decided to make it illegal. This decision set an important precedent that continues to have an impact today. There is no public record available regarding the debate that took place over the bill or even what the vote count was on the bill.

Marijuana laws in the state of Nebraska are no longer based on the original legislation, which is not mentioned in the current statutes. Despite its role in setting the path for policy, the original piece of legislation has seemingly dissipated like a forgotten memory.

Although Nebraska was among the group of states that outlawed cannabis prior to the 1937 Marijuana Tax Act it was, paradoxically, one of the first states that reduced the penalty for simple possession. Nebraska was one of eleven states that decriminalized marijuana in the 1970s. Decriminalization means that although marijuana is still illegal, simple possession of the substance is not treated as a serious criminal offense. Possession of under an ounce of marijuana is treated in the same manner as a traffic violation. Possession of more than one ounce but less than a pound of marijuana is a minor criminal offense that has a potential for some jail time. Possession of a pound or more is a felony and intent to sell any amount is also a felony. Under these regulations marijuana is certainly not legal, but the penalties are lighter in Nebraska than in some other states.

In 2000 and 2001, Senator Ed Schrock introduced legislation to allow legal cultivation of hemp, not marijuana, in Nebraska. The bill violated existing DEA

SESSION LAWS

Laws Passed by the

LEGISLATURE OF THE STATE OF NEBRASKA

at the

FORTY-FOURTH SESSION, 1927

which Convened in the

City of Lincoln, Nebraska

Tuesday, January 4th and Adjourned April 23, 1927

Compiled and Published by
FRANK MARSH
Secretary of State

393

MISCELLANEOUS

CHAPTER 145.

House Roll No. 74

INTRODUCED BY REPRESENTATIVES THOMAS AXTELL AND HENRY P. HANSEN OF LINCOLN

AN ACT to prohibit and regulate the importation, use and possession of Cannibas; prescribing penalties for the violation thereof; and to declare an emergency.

Be it Enacted by the People of the State of Nebraska:

Section 1. **Cannibas, Importation of.**—It shall be unlawful to import into the State of Nebraska cannibas, also known as hashish and mariguana, in any form or any preparation or derivative thereof: Provided, that cannibas, also known as hashish and mariguana, may be imported for medicinal purposes only, and then only by licensed pharmacists, licensed physicians and licensed veterinarians of the State of Nebraska.

Section 2. **Penalty.**—If any person shall fraudulently or knowingly import or bring into the State of Nebraska, or assist in so doing, any cannibas or any preparation or derivative thereof contrary to law, or shall receive, conceal or in any manner facilitate the transportation or concealment of such cannibas or preparation or derivative thereof, after importation, such cannibas or preparation or derivative thereof shall be forfeited, and shall be destroyed, and the offender shall be fined in any sum not exceeding Five Hundred ($500.00) Dollars and not less than One Hundred ($100.00) Dollars, or by imprisonment in the penitentiary for any time not exceeding three (3) years and not less than one (1) year, or both.

Section 3. **Planting and Cultivation Unlawful.**—It shall be unlawful for any person, association or corporation within this State to plant, cultivate, produce, sell, barter, or give any cannibas, be it known by whatever name, or preparation or derivative

regulations and did not pass in either session.

In late 2014, Nebraska and Oklahoma filed a lawsuit in the U.S. Supreme Court against Colorado, alleging that Colorado's legalization of marijuana violated the U.S. Constitution because federal law still prohibits cannabis possession. Nebraska and Oklahoma argue that their enforcement costs have increased because of Colorado's actions. In 2015, citing a host of constitutional, legal and practical problems, U.S. Solicitor General Donald Verrilli urged the Supreme Court not to allow two states to sue Colorado directly over this issue. Colorado argued

it is not responsible for the behavior of individual purchasers. The state prohibits interstate commerce of the drug and requires background checks for growers and vendors. In March, 2016 the Court decided it would not hear the case.

In recent years, there has been an effort to legalize marijuana for medicinal purposes within the state. Senator Tommy Garrett proposed bill LB 643, the Cannabis Compassion and Care Act during the 2015 session of the Nebraska legislature. This bill would allow patients suffering from a select group of diseases to legally use medicinal marijuana. The proposed bill was stripped of many of its

central features once it left the committee and made its way to the floor. The amended bill would not actually allow marijuana to be smoked, it only allowed cannabis to be ingested as a liquid, pill or liquid vapor. The Nebraska legislature did not vote on the bill during the 2015 session. Senator Garrett proposed similar legislation in 2016, but once again it was unsuccessful.

A change in federal law regarding hemp has opened the door to hemp research in Nebraska. Section 7606 of the 2014 Farm Bill defines industrial hemp as distinct from marijuana and allows universities or a state department of agriculture

to conduct research and develop pilot programs in hemp cultivation. The individual state must authorize this action before research can begin. Nebraska took this step when the Unicameral passed LB 1001 and it was signed by the governor in April 2014. LB 1001 stopped short of full hemp legalization, as the measure only makes hemp cultivation by universities legal for research purposes.

In May 2015, lawmakers gave the University of Nebraska Medical Center (UNMC) permission to use a cannabis extract called cannabidiol to treat people with intractable epilepsy. Medical marijuana will be available in Nebraska on a limited basis under LB 390. The bill creates a pilot study at UNMC to allow access to low-tetrahydrocannabinol (THC) oil for patients who suffer intractable or treatment-resistant seizures. Practitioners, patients and their parents participating in the study are exempt from prosecution for possession of a controlled substance. The study will designate at least two physicians to conduct research on the safety and preliminary effectiveness of cannabidiol use. The physicians are responsible for determining patient eligibility for participation in the study.

As cannabis laws change in other states, Nebraska will likely revisit issues of hemp cultivation, medical marijuana, and recreational marijuana use many times in the coming years.

Hemp Biology

Cannabis: A Botanical Snapshot

Steven J. Rothenberger, PhD

Professor of Biology, retired University of Nebraska Kearney

Introduction

Hemp (*Cannabis sativa* L.) is a member of a small plant family (Cannabaceae) that contains only 2 genera and 3 species of aromatic herbs in all of North America. These two genera (or groups) of plants are *Cannabis* (hemp) and *Humulus* (hops). Both genera are of ethnobotanical interest because they are associated with human intoxicants but in quite different ways. Morphologically, they hardly resemble relatives. Hops is a widely distributed vine in the temperate Northern Hemisphere.

The female flowers are contained in cone-like structures that are cultivated, harvested, and utilized as a flavoring and stabilizing agent in beer during the brewing process. The term "hops" is both a common name for this plant and a reference to the individual female cones.

Hemp is a tall, glandular, aromatic herb that can grow as high as 6 m. The plants are also dioecious meaning they occur as separate sexes. "Male" and "female" plants contain flowers that differ structurally. Staminate (or male flowers) produce the pollen that contains sperm cells, and pistillate or female flowers house the egg cells within the ovaries. The plants are wind-pollinated. Even though the male plants yellow and die in early autumn, they are a significant source of allergenic pollen. The female plants remain dark green much later and can continue to grow in high-quality soils. The leaves are the most recognizable structural feature and appear on a wide variety of objects, such as t-shirts, flags, notebooks, window stickers, etc. They have a palmated compound shape which means that the leaflets diverge outward from a central point resembling the palm of the hand.

Taxonomy

The taxonomy of hemp is not well-defined as it is occasionally the subject of disagreement among biologists. Some taxonomists split C. *sativa* into two subspecies. The low narcotic, wild, or escaped plants are placed in the subspecies sativa (as in Cannabis sativa L. subsp. *sativa*), while the subspecies *indica* (as in *Cannabis sativa* L. subsp. *indica*), contains higher levels of narcotic (Small and Cronquist 1976). Further complications occur when other plant scientists place *Cannabis* and *Humulus* in the mulberry family (Moraceae) which greatly expands the number of so-called "related" species. Small (1997) concludes that *Cannabis sativa* should suffice for all plants encountered in North America. Others argue that *Cannabis* is at a minimum a polytypic species because of its long history of cultivation

and manipulation by humans. (Polytypic means that this species consists of many varieties or "types".) In fact, a number of hybrids have been produced that vary as to their fiber content and the kinds of phytocannabinoids (CBDs) they contain. CBDs are chemicals that possibly have medicinal value. Examples of these hybrids are the industrial fiber varieties: "Fehling 34", "Kompolty", "Zolo 11", "Zolo 15" and the medicinal varieties: "HP Mexican", "MX", and "W1".

The Flora of Nebraska (2013) lists 5 common names for C. *sativa* including ditchweed, grass, hemp, marijuana, and pot. Modern usage of terms does distinguish between hemp and marijuana. Hemp refers to the low THC (tetrahydrocannabinol), escaped,

domesticated plants grown mostly for fiber. Marijuana most often is used to describe the illicit, drug-laced plants sold on the black market. Additional common names for these plants are reefer, joint, and Mary Jane. To further complicate the issue, since 1970 *Cannabis* of all types has been labeled as a Schedule 1 narcotic, illegal to grow, buy, sell and possess. This classification has hampered pharmaceutical and agronomic research and even places legitimate fiber growers at risk of prosecution.

Distribution

Hemp is one of the oldest cultivated plants, as it was grown for centuries as a source of fibers and later for its narcotic resins. The plant was introduced into

North America as early as 1630 and was widely cultivated for the manufacture of rope and cloth. Throughout the 19th century prior to 1860, the states of Kentucky, Missouri, and Illinois had well-established hemp industries producing tens of thousands of tons annually (Dodge 1896). From 1860-1895, the U.S. market gradually declined as a result of competition with high quality hemp imported from the Philippines and a general decline in shipbuilding. The low-narcotic, weedy hemp plants found throughout the Great Plains are the escaped descendants of these cultivated crops. This species grows aggressively in waste places, open woods, vacant lots, and along roadsides, trails, and rails.

The Plants Database (USDA 2015) reports that hemp is widely distributed throughout the United States with the exception of Alaska, Hawaii, and Nevada. *The Flora of North America* (1993) illustrates the principle naturalized range of this introduced species which is confined to the central and eastern one-fourth of the lower 48 states, restricted in the west by dry conditions and less fertile soil. Therefore, in the Great Plains, it is more common in the east than in drier, western counties and states. In the Nebraska Panhandle, hemp has been recorded in only 4 out of 11 counties and in 8 out of 27 counties in the western one third of the state (Kaul et al. 2013). Nebraska's earliest documented collections are from Douglas (1877), Lancaster (1887),

Sheridan (1889) and Brown (1897) Counties. The University of Nebraska at Kearney Herbarium collection contains 57 *Cannabis* plants many of which were collected in 1982 by students. The oldest documented *Cannabis* plants at the University of Nebraska at Kearney include one collection at Kearney by M.J. Hendickson, 15 August 1934, and a collection by an unknown collector at Kendrich, Oklahoma on 19 July 1905.

Physiology

Hemp is a short-day plant, flowering in response to shorter days and longer nights of late summer. At latitudes closer to the equator, plants flower later than those found at temperate latitudes. Generally, these plants contain higher level of phytocannabinoids (CBDs) than those growing to the north. CBDs are a class of terpenophenolic compounds that accumulate in the glandular trichomes (hairs) of the plant. At least 110 different CBDs have been discovered in *Cannabis* plants (Chandra *et* al. 2013) but research data are lacking for most. The glandular hairs on the leaf and stem surfaces are a source of resin that contains CBDs including the narcotic THC. Naturalized hemp in North America is mostly derived from temperate European and Chinese fiber strains that are ill adapted to growing under environmental conditions present in the Southeastern U.S. The flowers, stem, and leaf surfaces of female plants generally contain higher levels of CBDs than do the males.

The oldest hemp specimen in the UNK collection, dating from 1905

Cannabis thrives, reaching its maximum height in moist, fertile soils, especially in areas that have been disturbed, along fence rows, or in roadside ditches. Optimal growth rates are reached on high–nitrogen soils typical of well-manured former feedlots. As a cultivated crop, hemp helps regenerate and detoxify the soil (Hemphasis 2015). For these reasons, the plant is an excellent candidate for crop rotation with small grains or even corn. Potential growers should check with their local cooperatives or hemp-growers organizations for marketing information.

In the Great Plains. hemp's natural range corresponds somewhat with the rainfall belt (1218 in.; 3146 cm) of the Shortgrass Prairie to the west and the Mixedgrass Prairie to the east (1828 in.; 4671 cm). As rainfall amounts decrease and soil quality declines, hemp is much less common. Soil texture and nutrient value are also important. Based on particle size, soil can be classified, from the largest to the smallest, as sandy, clay, or silty. Sandy soil or extremely compacted clay soils are problematic especially during the seedling stage. Loam is an optimal mixture of clay, sand, and silt because it provides air circulation, proper drainage, and fertility. Depending on the ratio of these components, various soil classifications are applied, such as sandy-loam, silty loam, etc. Medium loam is ideal for growing *Cannabis* as it is nutrient-rich and well drained, but does not dry out too quickly.

Hemp is a C3 plant meaning that it does not have high-efficiency photosynthesis. C4 plants with high-efficiency photosynthesis convert carbon dioxide to carbohydrate more rapidly than C3 plants. C4 plants, such as corn (*Zea mays*) and sugar cane (*Saccharum sp.*) with high-efficiency photosynthesis, grow best at 90-95° F (Betts 2015). However, many C3 plants such as hemp, smooth brome (*Bromus inermis*), dandelion (*Taraxicum officinale*), and musk thistle (*Carduus nutans*), are aggressive invaders sometimes difficult to control. Although its optimum temperature range is 65-75° F, hemp demonstrates significant growth during hot summer days typical of the northern Great Plains. Annual plants with a fibrous root system, this species reduces the loss of topsoil caused by wind erosion. Some growers claim successful

yields on marginal soils. Because of its highly competitive growth rate, it tends to shade and crowd out many weedy species. This effect reduces the overall cost of production by eliminating or reducing the use of herbicides.

References

Berry J.A. and O. Björkman. 1980. Photosynthetic response and adaptation to temperature in higher plants. Annual Review of Plant Physiology 31:491–543.

Betts, D.L. 2015. "What is the difference between C3 and C4 plants?"

Kansas State University Research and Extension. www/midway.kstate.edu

Chandra, S., H. Lata, I. Khan, and M. ElSohly. 2013. The role of biotechnology in Cannabis sativa propagation for the production of phytocannabinoids. p. 123148 In S. Chandra, H. Lata and A. Varma (eds). Biotechnology for medicinal plants. SpringerVerlag. Berlin, Heidelberg. 464 pp.

Dodge, C.R. 1896. Hemp culture. P. 215222 In Morton, J.S. (Sec.). Yearbook of the U.S. Department of Agriculture, U.S. Government Printing Office, Washington, DC. 656 pp.

Haney A. and F.A. Bazzaz. 1970. Discussion. In Joyce, C.R.B. and S.H. Curry, eds. The botany and chemistry of Cannabis. Churchill, London.

Hemphasis. 2015. www.hemphasis.net/Environment/environment.htm

Kaul, R.B., D. M. Sutherland, and S.B. Rolfsmeier. 2013. The flora of Nebraska (2nd ed.). Conservation and Survey Division, Institute of Agriculture and Natural Resources. University of Nebraska, Lincoln. 966 pp.

Miller, N.G. 1970. The genera of the Cannabaceae in the southeastern United States. Journal of the Arnold Arboretum 51:185203.

Small, E. and A. Cronquist. 1976. A practical and natural taxonomy for Cannabis. Taxon 25:405435.

Small, E. 1997. Cannabaceae. In Flora of North America Editorial Committee, eds. 1993+. Flora of North America North of Mexico. 19+ vols. New York and Oxford. Vol. 3 pp. 381387.

USDA. 2016. Plants database. www//plants.USDA.gov/

Soil and Nutrient Requirements for High Quality Industrial Hemp

Raymond C. Ward, PhD
Ward Laboratories

Hemp is an adaptable plant, and is grown in a variety of environmental conditions around the world. However, the common myth that "hemp will grow anywhere" is simply not true. In general, hemp grows best in fertile, well-drained loam or finer textured soils that are well aerated. A useful rule of thumb is that industrial hemp will grow wherever corn and wheat are successfully grown. While hemp can be grown in other areas, the plant seems best adapted to the same climate and soils which support high quality corn and wheat production.

Hemp does not prosper in sandy, low fertility soils or poorly-drained clay. Soils with poor or limited internal drainage are not suited to hemp cultivation because the newly-emerged seedlings are susceptible to damping off disease. Damping off disease refers to the mortality caused by a number of soil-borne pathogens that kill seedlings shortly after germination. Young plants are also very sensitive to wet soils or flooding for the first three weeks, or until the plant reaches the fourth internode stage of growth. The water damaged plants are slow to recover, and produce lower yielding fiber or seed harvests. The physical properties of the soil should exhibit good structure for root development and water movement. Compacted soil limits root growth and restricts water movement which impacts the eventual yield of fiber and seed.

Industrial hemp needs adequate spring moisture for germination and steady summer moisture during flowering and seed set. Therefore, hemp growers should utilize areas with adequate natural rainfall and soils with high water holding capacity. Lower-rainfall areas with good soil can be used if irrigation is available. Hemp's total water requirement during the growing period, 20 to 28 inches, does vary with local climate and weather. Since hemp is adapted to corn and wheat growing areas it seems reasonable to assume that the water requirement must be roughly similar to wheat or corn. Total annual rainfall is only part of the story though, water availability during germination, early growth, flowering and seed set is critical. Seeds germinate early, after soil temperature rises above 41 degrees. Thus, spring rains are vital to production. Hemp is a short-day plant, and begins to develop flowers one month after the summer solstice. About one half of the total water requirement is needed during flowering and seed set, so adequate moisture in July and August has a profound impact on harvest. Given these growth characteristics, sandy soils in areas with limited midsummer rains and no irrigation are not suited to hemp production.

Another common myth is that hemp does not require any fertilizers. In reality, industrial hemp fertility needs are very similar to the fertility needs of corn or wheat, and consistent production requires an adequate supply of plant nutrients. Industrial hemp harvests are highest when the soil has high levels of organic matter. Soil tests should be taken before planting to assess the nutrient profile of the soil. Industrial hemp grows best when soil pH is slightly alkaline. If soil pH is 5.5 or less the soil should be limed to neutralize acidity and to bring soil pH to 7.0. The best method to determine liming rates is

a buffer pH soil test. This test measures total acidity that needs to be neutralized by the liming process. General nitrogen application rate will vary from 40 to 180 lbs of N per acre depending on soil nitrate values, yield potential of hemp, and past legume crop or manure application. A good guide is 0.1 lb of N per lb of seed production minus the other N sources just mentioned.

Phosphate application rate depends on phosphorus (P) soil test value. Phosphate needs for a low test is about 60 lbs of P_2O_5 per acre, medium test is about 30 lbs of P_2O_5 per acre and high test no P_2O_5 is needed. Phosphate may be applied in many different methods. It is important to maintain an adequate level of each nutrient.

Potassium (K) application rate depends on the exchangeable K soil test. In the Great Plains many soils are well supplied with potassium so potash fertilizer is not needed. Further east, in the Corn Belt most soils will need some potash fertilizer. Low K soil test values need 60 to 70 lbs of K_2O per acre. Medium K soil test values will require 20 to 35 lbs of K_2O per acre. High soil tests will not need additional potash. Sulfur (S) is another nutrient that is needed in many soils. It is a good idea to apply some sulfur with the nitrogen application. A ratio of 6 parts N to 1 part S is a good practice to use where sulfur is needed. Micronutrients are needed in the same amounts as wheat or corn.

At the current time, no pesticides are registered for use on hemp in the United States. To minimize the impact of pests or disease, systematic rotation of crops is a very good practice. Industrial hemp should be grown only once in a 4 year cycle. To avoid hemp diseases, do not plant hemp after canola, edible beans, soybeans, or sunflowers.

Suggested Readings:

Baxter, J. 2000. Growing Industrial Hemp in Ontario. Agdex# 153/20. Available at http://www.omafra.gov.on.ca/english/crops/facts/00067.htm#fertility

Purdue University: The Hemp Project. https://purduehemp.org/hempproduction/

Hemp Technologies Collective. www.hemptechnologies.com/page83/page83.html.

A Growing Guide for Industrial Hemp Farmers. https://australianhempparty.com/page/cultivation/growingguide.

Hemp Adds to the Profitability of Corn-Soybean Rotation

Frank Tenkorang, PhD

Professor of Agribusiness University of Nebraska Kearney

Many studies have been done on the benefits of low THC industrial hemp, particularly after Canada legalized production in 1998. This section looks at the profit feasibility of industrial hemp as an alternative crop when added to a corn-soybean rotation. In Nebraska, corn is king. Corn has been grown in the state for over 1000 years; 18th century tribes lived on it, and now 21st century farmers make their living on it. Yields have increased from about 30 bushels per acre in the 18th century to 180 bushels per acre today, thanks to high yielding varieties and chemical fertilizers, especially nitrogen fertilizer. A major concern for environmentalists is the potential harmful effect of inorganic fertilizers on the environment. To reduce the use of chemical fertilizer, and thus address this environmental concern, king corn has a valuable friend - soybeans. The benefits of corn-soybean rotation, including an increased corn yield and reduced production costs due to nitrogen fixation of soybean are well documented. In Nebraska, the ratio of soybean-corn rotation acreage has increased from about 19% in 1980 to 36% in 2015, attesting to the importance of soybeans to corn. A corn-soybean rotation, however, has a noteworthy problem. While corn after soybean minimizes nitrogen fertilizer application, this benefit is eroded by the significant amount of chemicals needed to manage soybean cyst nematodes (SCN). SCN is a parasitic roundworm that attacks soybean roots thereby reducing yields. It is estimated that SCN can cause up to 30% yield losses, amounting to $1 billion a year in the United States. SCN is found in over 30 states, including Nebraska. Managing SCN is a daunting task because the nematodes are soil borne and cannot be eradicated. One way to manage SCN is to use resistant soybean varieties. However, this is not optimal because resistant varieties are associated with lower yields and over time SCN could overcome the resistance. This leaves crop rotation as the best management practice because rotating soybean with a non-host crop reduces the number of nematodes.

Hemp to the Rescue?

Farmers using crop rotation to manage SCN have a variety of crops to choose from, including alfalfa, sorghum, and wheat. Where hemp cultivation is legal, it makes an attractive rotational crop for several reasons. Hemp's extensive root system will break up dense soil, and its fallen leaves enrich the soil. Importantly, hemp thrives where corn and soybean thrive, thus making it a suitable candidate for rotation in Nebraska. A rotational

Alternating corn and soybeans increases farm profitability.

crop is only attractive if it improves profitability. Will rotating hemp with corn and soybeans improve farm profits? A variety of field studies have found that a one year planting of hemp reduces SCN by 50-80%, with an increased reduction in fields using hemp leaf compost. These studies show the potential of hemp in reducing the cost of soybean production. On the revenue side, demand for hemp products exists as the U.S. imported $500 million of hemp products in 2013[1]. Some of the U.S. firms using hemp in their production include, Ford Motors (automobile), arAna (clothing), and Dr. Bronner's Magic Soaps (detergent). Market data is sketchy in the U.S. due to the ban on industrial hemp production, therefore, studies have used Canadian prices and production data estimates to show the revenue potential from hemp seed and fiber.

Given the environmental benefits of hemp, its ability to reduce soybean production costs, and its revenue potential, a partial budget analysis was developed to determine hemp's attractiveness as an alternative rotational crop in a three-crop rotation with soybean and corn. The rotation assumes a three acre field previously used for corn and soybean production with 1.5 acres allocated to each crop. Table 1 shows the three-crop rotation for three years, with the following analysis based on the rotation in the second year. Subsequent

1 According to Globe Newswire as found in Agrinews (http://agrinewspubs.com/Content/News/MoneyNews/Article

years' rotations beyond the third year will follow in the same order.

Table 1. Corn-Soybean-Hemp Rotation

	Field 1	Field 2	Field 3
Year 1	Hemp	Corn	Soybeans
Year 2	Corn	Soybeans	Hemp
Year 3	Soybeans	Hemp	Corn

Hemp is grown for either fiber, seed or both. A 2013 hemp profitability study done in Kentucky assumed fiber yields range from 2.2 to 8.1 tons per acre while seed yields range from 520 to 1050 lbs per acre a year. The actual yield depends on soil productivity which was determined by corn yield. To be conservative, the medium-high productivity in that study which corresponds to 150 bushels per acre of corn is used in this analysis. These conservative yields are 7.0 tons/acre of fiber and 900 lbs of seeds if hemp is grown for only fiber and for only seeds, respectively. If hemp is grown for both seeds and fiber, the yields are much smaller, 3.3 tons/acre and 780 lbs/acre, respectively. The low dual production yields is due to the fact that both female and male plants are harvested in fiber only production but only female plants are available for harvest in dual production as the male plant would have died and withered before the seeds are ready for harvest. The partial budget analysis is done for the three scenarios: fiber only,

seed only, and both seed and fiber. In 2011, hemp seed price estimates in Canada were priced at 90 cents to a dollar per lb ($1US = C$1 in 2011). The Kentucky study used modest prices of 50 to 80 cents per lb. A 70 cents per lb is chosen for this analysis. Fiber price was assumed to be $75 per ton (from the 2013 Kentucky study). 2014 production cost of hemp was deduced from the relationship between corn and hemp production costs in 1993 (due to data availability). The partial budget (Table 2) accounts for 50% reduction in herbicide

use due to reduction in SCN as a result of soybean following hemp, and 25% reduction in nitrogen fertilizer use due to corn following soybeans.

Allocating some farm ground to hemp will change both the production cost and revenues for corn and beans. The farmer, like all successful business owners, makes decisions on the basis of net change. Rotating hemp with corn and soybeans is profitable in all three scenarios that were modeled – the net change for growing hemp for fiber, for growing seed only, and for dual production of fiber and seed were all positive. However, growing hemp for only seed is the most profitable. These results agree with the Kentucky study regarding the profitability of growing hemp for seed.

As of 2016, nine states have passed laws to allow hemp production under government supervision, with other states set to move forward once hemp is legalized by the federal government. If hemp-soybean-corn rotation is indeed profitable, then producers in the nine current production states are better positioned to benefit than those in the remaining states. Given the current momentum of hemp legalization, it is likely that additional states will soon allow cultivation. Nebraska policymakers now need to decide if Nebraska is going to be an early hemp legalization state or is going to ask its farmers to sit on the sidelines and arrive late to the party.

Table 2. Partial Budget: Hemp–Soybean–Corn Rotation

Positive Impacts				Competing Impacts			
	Production System				Production System		
Increased Incomes ($)	Fiber & Seed	Fiber only	Seed only	Increased Costs ($)	Fiber & Seed	Fiber only	Seed only
Hemp fiber, revenue per acre	247.50	525.00	0.00	Variable cost	469.76	456.08	242.91
Hemp seed, revenue per acre	546.00	0.00	630.00	Fixed cost	479.33	319.553	307.46
10% increase in corn yield[1]	60.18	60.18	60.18				
30% increase in soybean yield	156.53	156.53	156.53				
Total	1010.21	741.71	846.71	Total	949.09	775.63	550.37
	A	B	C		E	F	G

Reduced Costs ($)				Reduced Incomes ($)			
Soybean Herbicide reduction per acre 50%	13.915			Corn revenue: 0.5 acre	300.90		
Corn Nitrogen fertilizer reduction per acre 25%	39.195			Soybean revenue: 0.5 acre	277.19		
Corn production cost for 0.5 acres	360.645						
Soybean production cost for 0.5 acres	242.495						
Total	656.25			Total	578.09		
	D				H		

Total positive impacts (I)	1666.46	1397.96	1502.96	Total competing impacts (II)	1527.18	1353.72	1128.46
	A+D	B+D	C+D		E+H	F+H	G+H

Net Change (I – II)	139.28	44.24	374.50

1 – Corn: Price = $3.54 per bushel, Yield = 170 bushels; Soybeans: Price = $10.87, Yield = 51 bushels

Suggested Readings

Andy Kerr, The Environmental Benefits of Using Industrial Hemp. The Larch Company. (www.naihc.org/KerrIHbenefits.pdf)

Economic Considerations for Growing Industrial Hemp: Implications for Kentucky's Farmers and Agricultural Economy Department of Agricultural Economics, University of Kentucky, July 2013 (http://www2.ca.uky.edu/cmspubsclass/i lEconomicConsiderationsforGrowingIndustrialHemp.pdf)
USDA, ERS. Industrial Hemp in the United States: Status and Market Potential (http://www.ers.usda.gov/media/328262/ages001e_1_.pdf)

E.A. Laate, Industrial Hemp Production in Canada, Government of Alberta, Agriculture and Rural Development (http://www1.agric.gov.ab.ca/$department/deptdocs.nsf/all/econ9631

Hemp Industry Association Vote Hemp. Senators Wyden, Paul, Merkley and McConnell Introduce S. 359, a Bipartisan Senate Companion Bill to H.R. 525, the Industrial Hemp Farming Act (http://www.votehemp.com/PR/20130215vh_senate_hemp_bill_s.359.html)

University of Minnesota Extension, Soybean Cyst Nematode: Management Guide. (http://www.extension.umn.edu/agriculture/soybean/soybeancystnematode/EFANSSoybeanSoybeanCystNematodeWebQuality.pdf)

Hemp Farming. A rapidly growing industry. (http://savethefishhempoil.com/hempfarming/)

G. Scheifele, P. Dragla, C. Pinsonneault, and J.M. Laprise. 1996 Hemp Research Report, Kent County, Ontario, Canada. (http://www.hempworld.com/hempcyberfarm_com/htms/countries/canada/ontario/1996ontario01.html#10.21%20Soybean%20Cyst%20Nematode)

Hemp: A World of Diverse Cultivars

Shane Davis
Co-Owner, Bolder Hemp Farm

Through 10,000 years of purposeful cultivation, humans have created a vast array of differentiated hemp cultivars. As the plant spread from its Central Asia origin, growers sought to produce plants with desirable characteristics, like long, uniform fibers. Through selective breeding, strains were developed that were best adapted to the local growing conditions. Each industrial hemp variety has its own appearance and its own set of chemical characteristics. Hemp grown for fiber may look like a small tree - the now-extinct Kentucky variety grown until the 1940s could reach heights of nearly twenty feet. Some current East Asian strains are only six feet tall with a ten foot leaf spread. Hemp grown for seed is generally shorter than plants grown for fiber, but can produce up to one thousand pounds of seeds per acre. Depending upon the end-use in mind, existing cultivars can emphasize small or large seeds, the volume of seeds, higher or lower oil content, or different CBD/THC ratios. All hemp is Cannabis sativa L, but that does not mean that it all has the same chemical characteristics or morphology.

Because much of the hemp historically grown in Europe and western Asia was used to produce fibers for ropes and twine, there is a considerable mutual genetic similarities between the modern European and West Asia cultivars. The earliest hemp grown in Colonial America came from this Eurasian stock.

In the 1850's, new varieties of eastern Chinese broad-leave hemp were brought to the U.S., with several generations of crossbreeding with other strains subsequently leading to the development of the renown Kentucky cultivar. Unfortunately, the prohibition on cannabis cultivation in Western Europe and North America stifled cultivar development since the mid 1930s.

Legalization of hemp cultivation in Canada restarted the process of diversification in North America. Canadian farmers can only grow strains appearing on the official list provided each year by Health Canada. Farmers cannot grow common "ditchweed" seeds. The approved list has grown from 23 cultivars

in 1999 to 45 cultivars in 2015. Industrial hemp varieties tested in Ontario to date have all been of European origin, with the exception of new Ontario-bred varieties such as Anka and Carmen. The provision in the 2014 Farm Bill allowing individual states to authorize hemp research will surely lead to the development of new hemp varieties in the U.S.

Not only has the diversification of hemp restarted, it will surely accelerate as the global hemp market increases. Individual

hemp growers will seek to develop plants with increased cellulose content for biomass fuel production, higher primary fiber yields for pulping, or high yields of extra fine fibers for textiles. Seed growers and processors will target high yielding varieties with increased levels of valuable protein, omega fats, and CBD. Hemp geneticists will also try to improve the plant's common agronomic traits such as increased tolerance to drought, salt, cold, heat or humidity and resistance to pests and diseases. Researchers will try to develop strains that thrive in wet, heavy soils or sandy, low-nutrient soils. The race is on to expand hemp production beyond its present day range.

There are more exotic genetic possibilities on the horizon. Hemp varieties could be developed with instantly-recognizable morphological markers that would help agricultural inspectors or the DEA identify approved low THC varieties. Future hemp fields may be filled with red, yellow or purple plants, or plants with simple leaves rather than the well-known cannabis palmated compound leaf. Hemp grown for paper pulp may grow in a rainbow of colors, thereby producing a better color paper using less bleach during pulping.

A central question for the pioneer growers in the United States as hemp cultivation returns is: What are the desired phenotypes for the future of industrial hemp cultivars? A phenotype is the set of observable structural characteristics of an individual plant resulting from the interaction of its genotype with the environment. Every environment offers a unique set of parameters to live within such as, but not limited to; temperature, humidity, wind, nutrients, water, light, predators and much more. The external factors, or stimuli of the environment the plant lives in, shapes the way the plant responds as it adapts to the surrounding environment. Simply stated, this ever-changing bundle of environmental factors influence a plant's physical, genetic and chemical diversities.

The chemical diversity within a species is known as chemotypes. For hemp, the important chemotypes are defined by the content and composition of their CBD and the ratio of CBD to THC. Cultivated hemp is limited to THC levels of .3 percent or less, so has higher CBD to THC ratios than marijuana has. This chemical diversity is capturing increasing attention by plant geneticists as ongoing medical research is finding that cannabinoid compounds may have a number of medicinal uses.

There are three general desired phenotypes: seed, high CBD, and fiber. Below is a brief description of these phenotypes and their common uses.

Seed phenotype: Normally planted fairly densely, at seeding rates of 35 - 45 pounds of seeds per acre, plants grown for seed have shorter stalks and larger seed heads than other hemp. After pollination in midsummer, the flower produces its seeds. Harvesting occurs when 60 percent of the seeds are ripe, generally 100 - 120 days after planting. The 'seed phenotype' can produce up to one thousand pounds of seed per acre in ideal conditions. Hemp seed is considered one of the most nutritionally advanced seeds. They are used for making hempseed oil for food or hemp-hearts (shelled hemp seeds for food industry). Hemp seed oil can also be used to make paints and varnishes as well as hemp biodiesel fuel.

High CBD phenotype: Select breeding of high CBD hemp cultivars specifically for cannabinoid extraction which appear to offer a variety of health benefits without the THC psychoactive effect of medical marijuana. Cannabinoids are a class of diverse chemical compounds that act on cannabinoid receptors in cells that influence neurotransmitter release in the brain. Two of the best known high CBD varieties are Charlotte's Web (20 % CBD) developed in Colorado and Avidekel (15.8 - 16.3% CBD) from Israel.

Fiber phenotype: Characterized as tall, rapidly maturing, mostly limbless plants which are often monoecious (having both male and female reproductive organs on the same individual). Plants are closely spaced, with seeding rates of 50 - 60 pounds per acre. Harvest normally occurs 70 - 90 days after planting. This phenotype has been selected by generations of fiber-producing farmers to establish long even fibers through growth and maturation. Most fiber cultivars contain CBD as the primary cannabinoid and nearly zero THC (the principal psychoactive constituent of cannabis).

In discussing hemp variation, one would be remiss to omit the naturally occurring hemp commonly known as "ditchweed." The plant grows with great vigor and frequency from Nebraska and Kansas to the east coast. The existing plants trace their lineage back to the commercially grown hemp from colonial times through the Hemp for Victory program in World War II. Any disturbed soil along the edges of crop fields, railroads, highways, and fencerows will quickly fill with thousands of hemp plants. Birds love to eat the seeds, so new areas are continually colonized. Hemp does not tolerate high humidity, so ditchweed is less common in the southeastern states. And, while hemp has considerable drought tolerance, it does need moisture to germinate and to flower. Thus it is spotty in the arid West.

Because all cannabis was declared a Schedule 1 drug (most dangerous) by the 1970 Controlled Substances Act, universities have avoided any study of ditchweed. To collect samples would put a researcher at risk of fines or imprisonment. To study samples would require full security protocols that are prohibitively expensive. We find ourselves in a position then where we know very little about one of the most ubiquitous plants in our landscape. We know that ditchweed is well adapted to soils and growing conditions across its range, because it is prospering without any assistance from humans. We know that it grows without the benefit of herbicides,

> The effects of man's subconscious and later conscious selection for desirable characteristics combined with the effects of natural selection under the stress of new and sometimes inhospitable environments have acted significantly in morphologically and perhaps chemically altering the Cannabis plant. As a result, today, possibly some 10,000 years after the beginnings of the manhemp partnership, Cannabis has become one of the most variable of cultivated plants.
>
> Cannabis: An Example of Taxonomic Neglect
> Schultes, Klein, Plowman and Lockwood from
> Cannabis and Culture
> Vera Rubin, editor

pesticides, or synthetic fertilizer. We can know, with a fair amount of certainty, that naturally occurring hemp is low in THC. If that were not the case, there would be massive illegal harvesting taking place each year. But there are important things that we do not know. How much genetic diversity is present in naturally occurring hemp? What is the chemical profile? What is the CBD/THC ratio?

These are important questions. Bringing the vigor and vitality of ditchweed to existing commercial cultivars might improve harvest yields and cut production costs. If existing strains have high CBD/THC ratios, hemp-based medicines might be cheaper and more accessible. For individual farmers, that ditchweed they have been mowing down year after year might be more valuable than their corn or soybeans. Until universities can study the naturally occurring hemp, we do not know what we actually have.

Processing Hemp for Fiber: Challenges and Opportunities

Tapan Chaterjee
Chief Technical Officer BastLab, LLC, an Omaha based company

Hemp has the potential to create new economic opportunities that are financially robust and environmentally sustainable. The breadth of consumer and industrial products created from the fiber, seeds, and oil of this ancient plant is staggering. By way of analogy, hemp is similar to petroleum in that it can be processed into a seemingly endless number of products. However, unlike oil, hemp is a rapidly renewable raw material. Hemp is an adaptive plant, able to grow in a variety of environments and soils. Growing hemp is only one part of its successful production, for after harvesting the plant must be processed to reach its full range of potential uses. Processing hemp for fiber applications presents both challenges and opportunities. Hemp fibers are used to manufacture a wide range of products, including textiles, ropes and nets, carpets and mats, brushes, and mattresses, in addition to paper and board materials.

The initial processing step in preparing hemp fiber is known as "retting," sometimes referred to as "degumming." This is a biological process which separates the fibers from the core of the stem and from each other through the decomposition of the surrounding cell walls. There are five types of retting: field (also known as dew), water, enzymatic, chemical and mechanical. All can be applied to hemp as well as other bast fiber plants, including jute, flax, and kenaf. Retting liberates and separates the individual fibers by breaking down the

Hemp grown for fiber can reach 18-20 feet tall.

States. After cutting, the stalks are allowed to lay in the field for 2 to 3 weeks. Microorganisms in the soil soften and degrade the pectinous substances that bind the fiber with other plant tissues. Some moisture is required for this microbial breakdown to occur, hence the common reference to field retting as dew retting. A dry period after the stalks are cut requires a longer time on the ground. The grower must monitor the process to ensure that the desired separation occurs, and must turn the stalks periodically to get uniform separation. Leaving the stalks on the ground too long will reduce fiber quality. Dew retting largely relies on indigenous soil fungi to colonize the stem/bast and to degrade pectin and hemicellulose (particularly the arabinose) by releasing polygalacturunase (PGase) and xylanase.

Strengths of Field Retting:
i. Environmentally friendly.
ii. Operationally well-known, long practiced by farmers in Europe.
iii. Low labor requirements
iv. Original fiber strength is not diminished
v. Enhances fertility of the land

Weaknesses of Field Retting:
i. Vagaries of weather and other exogenous factors can substantially reduce yields as well as negatively impacting the quality of the fiber (typically only coarse fiber is produced using field retting.)
ii. Constrained by time. Must be performed within a set window after

pectin which naturally cements adjacent cells within the plant stem. Pectin is a complex carbohydrate that is a key component of a plant's cell wall. Pectin, along with the other components of the cell wall, give a plant the ability to retain its structure while allowing the plant to grow.

The final quality, color, and tensile characteristics of hemp fiber are largely determined by the retting process approach used, control of conditions, and the duration of treatment. It is worth noting that at the present time there is no single method that can simultaneously

deliver optimum results in terms of shorter retting period, uniform fiber strength, fiber purity, low environmental impacts, and cost. With no single optimal solution, the strengths and weaknesses of each of these processes must be considered in the development of the hemp industry. The end use of the fiber is also a factor in determining the preferred retting process. For example, low-cost field retting may be appropriate when the final product only requires coarse hemp fibers.

Field (dew) retting was the most common process used in the historical production of hemp fiber in the United

harvest.

iii. Requires specialized equipment for turning the stalks.

iv. Gums and pectins are not fully separated from the fiber, requiring an additional processing step called decortication.

In water retting, the stalks are submerged in freestanding ponds or running streams for 7 to 14 days. Naturally occurring bacteria in the water decomposes the pectin, thus releasing the fiber. Workers, standing in the ponds or streams, then hand strip the fibers from the stalks. Most of the world's currently produced high quality hemp is water retted in China. Water retting presents a considerable environmental challenge because the water in a hemp retting pond has a very disagreeable odor and is toxic to people and animals at the end of the process.

Strengths of Water Retting:
i. Produces high quality, fine fibers. (The fiber has very little, if any, residually attached pectin. The fiber surface is smooth and undamaged.)
ii. Does not require expensive processing equipment.
iii. Enhances color.
iv. Easily spins into yarn.
v. Modifies fiber surface, improving subsequent dying and bleaching of the fiber.

Weaknesses of Water Retting:
i. Slow and low processing throughputs
ii. Labor intensive

iii. Poses health risks to individuals standing in stagnant ponds
iv. Demands large amounts of water
v. Effluent treatment is very expensive

Chemical retting treatments typically include the use of sodium hydroxide or sodium benzoate. After being stripped from the stalk in ribbon form, the fibers are placed in a chemical bath and left to cure for a period of time. The fibers are then neutralized with an acid, rinsed and dried. Where field and water retting takes days, or even weeks, chemical retting can separate the fibers in as little as one hour of treatment.

Strengths of Chemical Retting:
i. Typically produces fiber that is the most free of all noncellulosic material.
ii. Very fast relative to field or water retting.

Weaknesses of Chemical Retting:
i. Requires large capital outlays for equipment that is expensive to run.
ii. Labor intensive.
iii. Lowers the tensile strength of the processed fiber
iv. Causes the fiber color to darken, an undesired outcome for certain applications.
v. Creates costly environmental disposal challenges.
vi. Requires adherence to very demanding quality control protocols.

Ezymatic treatments attempt to imitate the microbial action that occurs when

degumming the stalks through dew or water retting. The enzymes colonize the stalks, breaking down the pectins and gums much as the microbes in the soil and the water do. Scientists have created enzymes from strains of fungus and microbes that attack pectins and gums in natural settings. Hemp stalks are introduced into large baths (enzymatic cultures), and when exposed to these cultures, the pectins and gums degrade. The temperature, pH, resident time, and inoculation size are set such that the retting process provides optimal fiber yield. Researchers continue to create and refine enzymes, searching for ones that are both effective and economically viable.

Strengths of Enzyme Retting:
i. Enzymatic process occurs in a more controlled environment, yielding a greater percentage of uniformly retted fiber
ii. Studies have found that enzymatic retting is the most suitable method to reduce the amount of lignin in bast fibers.

Weaknesses of Enzyme Retting:
i. Requires large capital outlay and is operationally expensive, largely due to the cost of the enzymes
ii. Creates effluent that is expensive to dispose

Mechanical retting removes the noncellulosic material purely by mechanical means. Typically, this involves a stripping action that peels the lignans and pectins away from the fiber. To date, the use of a mechanical action in isolation has not effectively removed 100% of the noncellulosic material, though some companies have developed equipment that can remove a substantial amount of noncellulosic material from the fiber.

Strengths of Mechanical Retting:
i. Is environmentally friendly.
ii. Depending on the mechanical system used and the degree of degumming required, it can be the most cost effective.

Weaknesses of Mechanical Retting:
i. To date, mechanical retting cannot produce a 100% degummed fiber.
ii. Depending on the equipment, fiber can be subject to physical damage, weakening its endapplication performance and processability.

As Nebraska positions itself to economically benefit from the reintroduction of industrial hemp, decision makers in the public and private sectors need to understand the means by which the plant is processed. When processed for its fiber, one of the primary processing steps as discussed involves removing the noncellulosic material from the fiber, a process known as degumming or retting. Pros and cons exist for the different means of retting hemp fiber. From an environmental perspective, water and chemical processes create substantial water quality issues. In a state that values clean water, these methods can only become viable if researchers find an effective water treatment strategy. Dew retting is environmentally benign, but requires specialized equipment and could be subject to the vagaries of weather and natural microbial action. A more cost effective enzymatic treatment and/or an improved mechanical retting process are likely to be the primary candidates for widespread use in Nebraska.

After the cultivation of all cannabis was effectively curtailed by the Marijuana Tax Act of 1937, there was very little scientific research in the United States on hemp processing. In the short run, the lack of an existing optimal retting process may impede the development of a robust hemp industry. However, the current state of limited knowledge also creates a host of opportunities for university researchers and private sector entrepreneurs. Someone is going to develop better retting techniques - and reap the subsequent economic rewards. Nebraska's climate and soils gives it the potential to become a hemp production powerhouse, and perhaps it will be a Nebraska-based researcher or entrepreneur who will develop the next breakthrough in retting.

Markets and Uses

Male and Female hemp in late summer, south central Nebraska

Hemp Markets: Today and Tomorrow

Allan Jenkins, PhD
Professor of Economics University of Nebraska Kearney

In a February 1938 article, *Popular Mechanics* magazine called hemp a "new billion dollar crop." Adjusted for inflation, a billion dollars in 1938 would equal $16.8 billion today. The article was optimistic about the development of the hemp market for three major reasons. One, technological advancements had made processing hemp more efficient and less labor intensive. Two, the plant characteristics made it easy to grow as a rotational crop. Three, hemp could be used in the production of literally thousands of products, from explosives to building materials. Unfortunately for the editors of *Popular Mechanics* the article hit the newsstands just after the Marijuana Tax Act effectively eliminated the domestic production of hemp.

While domestic production practically disappeared after the Tax Act, there was always a residual interest in hemp. When Canada allowed research cultivation in 1994, it created new interest in hemp as an alternative crop. This new interest prompted a number of studies from states and the federal government regarding the production capacity and market demand for domestically produced hemp.

The first of these efforts, *The Report to the Governor's Hemp and Related Fiber Crops Task Force*, was released by Kentucky in 1995. The report noted that hemp could be effectively grown in Kentucky, as demonstrated in the historical production records. Planting hemp would have positive environmental impacts because it would reduce soil erosion and it required less pesticide use than other crops. However, the overall tone of the report was generally pessimistic. It noted that the extraction and processing of hemp fibers for high-quality textiles was still more difficult than for cotton, and that hemp faced a number of low-cost alternatives in its other potential uses.

> Currently, established markets for hemp in the U.S. are generally limited to specialty/novelty textiles, oils, foods, paper and other materials. The specialized nature of this market does not require competition with other fiber sources. The potential market size is difficult to predict, but it is unlikely to support the large acreage of a major new field crop.
> – *The Report to the Governor's Hemp and Related Fiber Crops Task Force*

The second report, *Feasibility of Industrial Hemp Production in the United States Pacific Northwest*, was published by Oregon State University in 1998. It was similar in tone to the Kentucky report,

The University of Kentucky was an earlier leader in resuming domestic hemp production.
Photo by aceshot1/Shutterstock.com

The Oregon State Report was printed on Vanguard Hemp, a product of the Living Tree Paper Company, Eugene, Oregon. It is 25 percent hemp, 25 percent cotton, and 50 percent postconsumer waste. The long fibers from hemp significantly improve and extend the recyclability of the postconsumer wastepaper.

generally concluding that hemp would, at best, be a specialty crop grown on limited acreage. Unlike Kentucky, only parts of the Northwest would support hemp cultivation. The report determined that the temperature and soil requirements of hemp could best be met in the existing agricultural areas of the Columbia and Snake River basins and to a lesser extent in the lowland areas between the Coast Range and the Cascades from the Rogue Valley to Puget Sound.

> The climatic and soil requirements of hemp can be met in some agricultural areas of the PNW, however, hemp will almost certainly require irrigation to reliably maximize productivity in the region. The requirement for supplemental irrigation will place hemp in direct competition with the highest value crops in the PNW, limiting available acreage. Stem yields will have to be substantially higher than those previously recorded for hemp to be economically feasible in the PNW at current prices. It is unlikely that the investment needed to improve hemp production technology will be made until legislative restrictions are removed from the crop.

A 1998 report from the University of Kentucky Center for Business and Economics Research, *The Economic Impact of Industrial Hemp in Kentucky*, had a more positive tone than the earlier reports. The report noted that

the worldwide demand for hemp was increasing, imports of hemp into the U.S. were increasing, and various European countries were actively engaged in research to improve hemp genetics and production technology. The study compared 14 common Kentucky crops and found that hemp could be the third most profitable crop in the state (tobacco products ranked first and second). Further, the authors argued that traditional economic metrics might not be directly applicable to hemp because its wide array of uses makes it a unique commodity. The report estimated that expected demand for hemp would require 82,000 acres of cropland. There was a proactive tone to the study, offering three reasons why Kentucky should move forward with legalization. First, hemp could met the needs of Kentucky's horse industry by providing affordable animal bedding. Second, Kentucky's long growing seasons and favorable soils would create profitable yields per acre. Third, the authors argued that Kentucky would have a longterm advantage over other states in establishing the hemp industry if it was the first state to legalize production.

A third report in 1998, this one from The Institute for Natural Resources and Economic Development, North Dakota State University was titled *Industrial Hemp as an Alternative Crop in North Dakota* was also generally favorable. The report noted that North Dakota could have an initial advantage because a newly constructed multi-oil processing facility was capable of processing hemp seed.

Further, the report determined that there were a variety of market opportunities that would support hemp production. Hemp hurds were price competitive with wood chips, fine wheat straw, or other types of animal bedding. Hurds could also be a complement or substitute material in strawboard production. Finally, the report determined that certified seed production would be a profitable market opportunity.

> The industrial hemp world market consists of over 25,000 products in nine submarkets: agriculture, textiles, recycling, automotive, furniture, food/nutrition/beverages, paper, construction mate rials, and personal care. These products are made or manufactured from raw materials derived from the industrial hemp plant: fiber, hurds, and hemp seed/ grain.
> *-Industrial Hemp as an Alternative Crop in North Dakota*

The next major report, *Industrial Hemp in the United States: Status and Market Potential*, came from the U.S. Department of Agriculture Economic Research Service (ERS) in January 2000. This report focused on the amount of domestic production needed to fill the market demand for imported hemp and its close competitors in the fiber and oilseed markets. The tone of the report was conservative, with the conclusion that the domestic market could be served with only a few thousand acres, perhaps as low as 2,000. Even the high end of

the ERS estimate was only 250,000 acres nationally, which meant that a few hundred farms could completely meet domestic demand. The report also noted the volatility in the early years of Canadian production, and argued that the inherent uncertainty about long run demand for hemp products and the potential for oversupply discounted the prospects for hemp as an economically viable alternative crop for American farmers.

> Imports of raw hemp fiber have increased dramatically in the last few years, rising from less than 500 pounds in 1994 to over 1.5 million pounds for the first 9 months of 1999.
> *-Industrial Hemp in the United States: Status and Market Potential*

The wild swings in Canadian production seem to have temporarily decreased U.S. interest in hemp production after 2000. Thus, it is more

than a decade before two new major studies were published. In March 2013, the Congressional Research Service (CRS) released *Hemp as an Agricultural Commodity*. This report was updated in 2014 and 2015. The general tone of the report was that hemp production in the United States faced a number of substantial obstacles in the foreseeable future. However, the main obstacles were political and legal, not economic. According to CRS, the main obstacles facing the development of this potential market were U.S. government drug policies and DEA concerns about hemp production. Briefly, the DEA concern was that commercial cultivation would likely increase the production of high THC marijuana, thus complicating enforcement activities. DEA officials and other observers also expressed a belief that efforts to legalize hemp (and to legalize medical marijuana) were merely a front for organizations whose real aim was to see marijuana production legalized.

Economically, for CRS the major barrier to hemp production in the United States was the competition from other global suppliers. The total world market for hemp products remained relatively small. China, with 40 percent of global production, has a major influence on market prices and thus on the year-to-year profits of producers in other countries. Canada's head start in the North American market for hemp seed and oil also would also likely affect the profitability of the U.S. domestic

The general finding was that on highly productive land hemp returns beat corn returns if the market price for corn was less than $6.00 per bushel. Estimated net returns were much better for oilseed production compared to fiber production. Fiber-only production showed a negative return in almost all of the scenarios evaluated. The seed only production had better returns than the dual fiber-seed system in all scenarios evaluated.

> Despite different assumptions and methodologies, our budget projections appear fairly consistent with other studies, generally indicating that hemp seed production can compete with the profitability of mainstream grain crops under the upper range of our hemp seed yield and price levels.
>
> ~Economic Considerations for Growing Industrial Hemp: Implications for Kentucky's Farmers and Agricultural Economy.

Estimating market demand for infant industries is always problematic. In calculating potential returns for hemp producers in Kentucky, the 2013 report noted that both hemp fiber and oilseed prices are highly uncertain, and thus uses a wide range of prices to measure potential profitability. Based on the results of the current state studies, it appears that the greatest near-term profit opportunity for U.S. farmers lies with growing seed for the food and cosmetic industries. Hemp grown for oil seed allows producers to also serve the specialized bird seed market.

industry. While recognizing these substantial obstacles, the CRS report ends with a positive assessment for the future development of the industry.

> Nevertheless, the U.S. market for hemp-based products has a highly dedicated and growing demand base, as indicated by recent U.S. market and import data for hemp products and ingredients, as well as market trends for some natural foods and body care products. Given the existence of these small-scale, but profitable, niche markets for a wide array of industrial and consumer products, commercial hemp industry in the United States could provide opportunities as an economically viable alternative crop for some U.S. growers.
>
> ~Hemp as an Agricultural Commodity

Kentucky's ongoing interest in legalizing hemp production created a third state report in 2013, *Economic Considerations for Growing Industrial Hemp: Implications for Kentucky's Farmers and Agricultural Economy*. Like the earlier studies, the report created a set of production/price scenarios then compared the profitability of hemp to a corn/soybean rotation.

Late summer male plants wither and die.

Further, the seed can be crushed for oil used in the production of biodiesel or other products.

Some people will buy hemp apparel and related items simply because they are made from hemp. This is probably a small but stable component of demand. A more volatile component is based on fashion trends and whether designers use hemp or linen-containing fabrics in their designs. In the last few years, some famous designers, including Calvin Klein, Giorgio Armani, and Ralph Lauren, have included hemp fabrics in their clothing lines.

One indicator of market potential is the annual change in the amount of hempbased products imported into the U.S. over time. For imported products, available statistics have only limited breakouts or have only recently been expanded to capture hemp subcategories within the broader trade categories for oilseeds and fibers. However, even with the recognized data limitations, the trend is unmistakable the value of imported hemp products is increasing. The earlier discussed CRS report estimates that the value of imported hemp seeds and fibers used in further manufacturing increased more than sixfold from 2005 to 2014.

The single largest supplier of U.S. imports of raw and processed hemp fiber is China. Other leading suppliers include Romania, Hungary, and India. The single largest source of U.S. imports of hemp seed and oilcake is Canada. The total value of Canada's exports of hemp seed to

the United States has grown significantly in recent years following resolution of a legal dispute over U.S. imports of hemp foods in late 2004. The United Kingdom and Switzerland also export hemp seed and oilcake to the U.S.

A third potential growth area for hemp is the bioenergy sector. Ethanol can be produced from the cellulose in hemp fiber, but the cellulosic ethanol industry continues to lag expectations for commercial success. Further, it is not clear whether hemp has any advantages over other cellulosic energy crops being considered, such as switch grass. The two share many of the same potential environmental benefits, but there is a much longer research experience in switch grass production (at least in the U.S.) and its conversion to energy.

As noted earlier, recent work implies that industrial hemp production could be competitive with other crops grown by U.S. farmers. However, this is largely based on speculation, due to the lack of an up-to-date U.S. research base on industrial hemp production. There are several lines of research that must be developed to have a better understanding of the commercial possibilities and profit potential for the commercial hemp industry. For example, one important area of research is cultivar development and selection for specialized production of seeds, fiber or CBDs. Since there has been no recent commercial production in the U.S., there has been little work on the development of cultivars for various U.S.

production environments. There has been some cultivar development in Canada, but varieties grown there may not provide the greatest production potential in much of the U.S. The provisions of the 2014 Farm Bill allowing universities and state departments of agriculture to grow hemp for research purposes has started a trickle of scientific breeding for desirable characteristics.

Even after the enactment of the 2014 farm bill provision allowing the cultivation of industrial hemp by research institutions and state departments of agriculture, the legal status of hemp production was still murky. For example,

Kentucky passed the enabling legislation and very publicly announced plans for several pilot projects through the Kentucky Department of Agriculture. Nevertheless, on May 13, 2014, a shipment of 250 pounds of viable hemp seed from Italy was blocked by U.S. Customs officials at Louisville International Airport. DEA officials contended the seizure was legal because the "importation of cannabis seeds continues to be subject to the Controlled Substances Imports and Export Act (CSIEA)," which restrict persons from importing viable cannabis seed unless the person is registered with DEA and has

obtained the necessary Schedule I research permit. Viable seeds refer to seeds that are alive and have the potential to germinate and develop into normal reproductively mature plants, under appropriate growing conditions. The DEA has allowed the importation of hempseed, but required that seeds be either heat sterilized or steam sterilized to remove any naturally occurring traces of THC. These processes make the seeds mostly incapable of germination.

To secure release of the hemp seeds, the Kentucky Department of Agriculture (KDA) filed a lawsuit in U.S. District Court against the DEA, the Justice Department, U.S. Customs and Border Protection, and the U.S. Attorney General. In the lawsuit, Kentucky argued that its efforts to grow industrial hemp are authorized under both state and federal law, and that the DEA should not seek to impose "additional requirements, restrictions, and prohibitions" on hemp production beyond requirements in the 2014 farm bill, or otherwise interfere with its delivery of hemp seeds.

Following a hearing before the U.S. District Court in Louisville, DEA issued a registration and import permit to KDA, allowing the state agency to possess the seeds. The Italian seeds were released to the state on May 23. But DEA still made it clear in a letter on May 22 that it had plans "to criminally prosecute and seize, under the federal Controlled Substances Act ... hemp plants grown by the private farmers who have entered

DEA agents seized a shipment of 250 pounds of viable seeds - prompting the Kentucky Department of Agriculture to file a lawsuit to obtain release of the seeds.

written contracts with KDA to carry out the pilot projects." After a series of negotiations, the seeds were eventually released and planted, and no private farmers participating in pilot projects with the KDA were raided.

Congress was unhappy with the DEA actions, and enacted additional legislation to stop the agency from taking similar actions in the future. Both the House and Senate FY 2015 Commerce Justice Science appropriations bills contained provisions to block federal law enforcement authorities from interfering with state agencies and hemp growers, as well as to counter efforts to obstruct agricultural research. The enacted FY 2015 appropriation includes a provision stating that "none of the funds made available" to the U.S. DOJ and the DEA "may be used in contravention" of the 2014 farm bill.

Hemp: One Plant, 25,000 Uses

For centuries, hemp was a source of fiber and oilseed used to produce a variety of textile, rope, and food products. Over time, an expanded menu of industrial and consumer uses were developed, with several sources now estimating that hemp has as many as 25,000 potential uses. Currently, more than 30 nations grow industrial hemp as an agricultural commodity sold on the world market. Cultivar selection plays a large role in hemp cultivation. Each variety of hemp has its own unique set of characteristics, producing small or large seeds, various

oil levels, different oil compositions, and differing fiber content. Growers seek the best cultivar based upon the desired end result and the growing conditions in the location the crop is grown.

In the U.S. hemp research and product development have been hampered because all cannabis was considered a Schedule I (most dangerous) narcotic after passage of the Controlled Substances Act (CSA) in 1970. Despite a variety of legitimate industrial and nutritional uses, hemp production was controlled and regulated by the U.S. Drug Enforcement Administration (DEA). The CSA did not make growing hemp illegal; rather, it placed strict standards governing the security conditions under which the crop was grown. These security standards were so costly that they effectively prohibited any legal cultivation. Until recently, a grower had to get permission from the DEA to grow hemp or face the possibility of federal charges or property confiscation, regardless of whether or not the grower had a state-issued permit.

The combination of state legalization of cultivation, the recognized distinction between hemp and marijuana in the 2014 Farm Bill, and the prohibition on federal interference through the 2015 budget now allows expanded research and development of hemp-based products in the U.S. One of the most exciting areas is in the exploration of hemp CBD-based medicines for humans and animals. Nutritionists are developing new consumer food products to take advantage

of hemp seed protein and antioxidants. Chemists and industrial engineers are developing new plastics, lubricants, and building materials with hemp.

Hemp Seed Products

Food

The DEA, with its responsibility to regulate controlled substances, approved a rule in March 2003 deeming all materials, compounds, mixtures and preparations with any amount of THC a Schedule 1 controlled substance. The agency's official position was that any THC containing substances are not fit for human consumption, no matter how small the THC level. This rule effectively made the sale of all hemp food products

Some hemp strains can produce 5 pounds of seed per plant.

Hemp seed

Nutrition Facts

Serving Size 100g

Amount Per Serving

Calories 580	Calories from Fat 423

	% Daily Value*
Total Fat 45g	69%
Saturated Fat 3g	17%
Cholesterol 0mg	0%
Sodium 0mg	0%
Total Carbohydrate 7g	2%
Dietary Fiber 3g	13%
Sugars 0g	
Protein 37g	

Vitamin A	0%	Vitamin C	0%
Calcium	0%	Iron	53%

*Percent Daily Values are based on a 2000 calorie diet. Your daily values may be higher or lower depending on your calorie needs.

illegal in the US. However, in February 2004, the Ninth Circuit Court of Appeals ruled that the DEA could not regulate hemp products because hemp was not a scheduled drug under the definitions of drugs in the Controlled Substances Act. The Court ruled that the DEA could only ban the presence of marijuana or synthetic THC. As a result of this ruling, food products containing sterilized industrial hemp seeds and/or oils could be sold legally in the US.

Hemp seed, which has a nutty flavor, is used in food and nutrition products similar to the way soybeans, poppy seed, or sesame seeds are used. The seeds contain 20-25 percent high quality protein, which makes them very nutritious. Currently in the U.S., hemp seed is found in granola, snack/protein bars, pretzels, yogurts, cheeses, beer, body-building supplements, and ice cream. Roasted or sterilized seeds are found in niche markets, such as natural food and specialty foods outlets. A variety of internet outlets sell whole seeds (approximately $4.00 per pound) or shelled hemp hearts (approximately $10 per pound). The overall market potential for hemp seed as an ingredient in food is unknown; however it is growing. Industrial hemp production statistics for Canada indicate that one acre of plants yields an average of about 700 pounds of seed, which can be pressed into about 50 gallons of oil and 530 pounds of meal.

In addition to its benefits for human consumption, hemp seed is a very valuable feed for different types of birds ranging from small songbirds, to doves and pigeons, to chickens and turkeys. A 1931 report from the Ukraine noted that in regions where hemp production was intensive, chickens were distinguished by higher egg laying and lower mortality from common diseases. In the United

Kingdom, there is an ongoing public campaign to "Feed the Birds" by scattering hemp seeds on idle public ground. The campaign's symbol is a member of the finch family known as a Common Linnet. The scientific name for the bird is Carduelis cannabina, derived from the species' extreme fondness for hemp seed.

As seeds are crushed for oil they create a seedcake that can be used for animal feed. A variety of studies have found hemp seedcake a quality livestock and poultry supplement. In trials comparing hempseed cake as a protein feed instead of soybean meal for growing cattle, results showed similar weight gain and carcass traits for both feeds, but an improved rumen function for hemp due to the higher content of fiber in hempseed cake in comparison to soybean meal. Recent trials in Kentucky reveal that hempfed cattle require less feed and digest it more efficiently.

Beer

There are a growing number of breweries in the United States now making hemp beer. Beer brewed with hemp, which is a botanical cousin to hops, can be sold in states which have not legalized marijuana as long as it tests negative for THC. A hemp beer's label cannot contain any slang or graphics "implying or referencing the presence of … marijuana" if it's going to be approved by the federal government for sale across state lines.

Edible oil

The use of hemp for edible oil dates back thousands of years. Its growing popularity is based upon increasing consumer awareness of its substantial nutritional benefits. Hemp oil has high levels of antioxidants, unsaturated fatty acids and protein. Hemp oil contains high levels of both linolenic (omega3) and linoleic (omega6) acids, two essential fatty acids. Linoleic and linolenic acids represent approximately 80% of its fatty acid composition. However, hemp oil has a limitation as an allpurpose kitchen oil it is generally unsuitable for frying or baking. The "smoke point" for hemp oil is only 320 degrees, very low in comparison with other oils like canola (400 degrees). A smoke point is the temperature at which an oil or fat gives off smoke. Heated past its smoke point, an oil starts to break down, releasing free radicals and a substance called acrolein, the chemical that gives burnt foods their acrid flavor and aroma. Smoking is an indicator the fats have turned rancid. Raw hemp oil has a limited shelf life, should be protected from direct sunlight and heat, and must be kept in dark colored bottles.

Non-Food Hemp Oil Consumer Products

Several products are made by crushing hemp seeds to obtain the oils. Existing personal care items include soap, shampoo, cosmetics, lip balm, insect repellent, lotions, and laundry detergent. European companies first introduced hemp oil-based personal care products in the 1990's. Hemp-based cosmetics and personal care products account for about half of the world market for hemp oil. The Body Shop, a British-based

international skin products company, began selling hemp products in the U.S. in 1998.

Hemp Fiber Products

Textiles

One of the reasons hemp fiber has been valued is because of its length. The primary bast fibers in the bark are 5–40 mm long, and are amalgamated in fiber bundles which can be 1–5 m long (secondary bast fibers are about 2 mm long). The woody core fibers are short—about 0.55 mm—and like hardwood fibers are cemented together with considerable lignin. The core fibers are generally considered too short for high grade paper applications (a length of 3 mm is considered ideal), and too much lignin is present. While the long bast fibers have been used to make paper almost for 2 millennia, the woody core fibers have rarely been so used. Nevertheless it has been suggested that the core fibers could be used for paper making, providing appropriate technology was developed. In any event, the core fibers, have found a variety of uses, as detailed below. The long, bast fibers also have considerable potential to be used in many non-paper, non-textile applications, as noted below.

Textiles made from hemp fibers include clothing, fine linen, yarn, upholstery, bags, sacks, tarpaulins, carpets and other home furnishings. Although many of these products are sold at high prices, hemp textiles have an appeal to a certain

part of the population who are willing to pay for the products (USDA 2000). Much of the hemp apparel that is found in the U.S. comes from yarns, fiber and fabrics that are imported from Europe or China. In addition to hemp apparel, home furnishings are also in demand, particularly in the "eco" friendly market. Environmentally friendly carpets and upholstery can be found in the private sector as well as the industrial sector.

Pulp and Paper

Hemp has always played a role in paper production, considering that the oldest surviving paper, over 2,000 years old, was made from hemp fiber in China. Until the early 19th century, hemp and flax were the chief papermaking materials. Woodbased paper came into use when mechanical and chemical pulping was developed in the mid 1800s in Europe. Currently, the pulp and paper industry relies on wood pulp, but some researchers have looked into the use of hemp pulp. While hemp based pulp was used in the past when producing conventional paper, recent analyses have concluded that this method is not profitable today. Current research in European countries has determined that hemp can be used as a fiber supplement to recycled paper due to its long fibers. Also, the European market has shown that there is a small niche for specialty hemp pulp products like cigarette paper and bank notes.

Plastic Composites

There are several products that can be made from hemp plastic composites, including fiberglass substitutes, injection molding, and press molded parts. Hemp fiber was first used in the production of plastic composites for use in automobiles by Henry Ford, and automobile components is the second most important part of the hemp industry in the E.U. In Europe, hemp fibers are used to reinforce trunk linings, rear decks, dashboards, headrests and door panels. Several small specialty companies in the U.S. have been outfitting vehicles such as buses with hempreinforced parts. The benefits from using hemp fibers in plastic composites include: weight reduction, positive results in crash tests, environmental benefits, occupational health benefits compared to glass fibers, and favorable mechanical, acoustical, and processing properties.

A World of Market Potential

The preceding paragraphs only touch the tip of hemp's total market potential. As cultivation increases, and as university researchers and entrepreneurs have an opportunity to evaluate all of hemp's special characteristics, the breadth and volume of hemp products will surely expand.

Industrial Hemp in Europe

William Aviles, PhD
Professor of Political Science University of Nebraska Kearney

While the politics around allowing the production of industrial hemp in Nebraska and the United States continues to evoke fierce debate and resistance from prohibitionists who view such production as opening the way for recreational cannabis, much of Europe settled these questions in the 1990s. After decades of European nations applying comparable restrictions upon hemp production, between 1993 and 1996 the cultivation of industrial hemp was legalized in most of the member states in the European Union. Production in Europe reached over 22,000 hectares (55,000 acres) of industrial hemp cultivated and processed in 2015—a record cultivation harvest in the thirty years that hemp began growing again in the region. All of this growth has happened, contrary to the expectations of prohibitionists in the U.S., without affecting the enforcement of marijuana laws. In fact, the European Union has successfully regulated THC levels in hemp flowers to 0.2%, undermining its use for the recreational cannabis market. The industry in fact seems readied for continued expansion and diversification in a variety of legal markets in the years to come while avoiding any rise of substance abuse.

Hemp Products and Markets

Industrial hemp had been grown in Europe for hundreds of years, through the Middle Ages and until the end of the sailing ship period with the strong hemp fiber being central to canvas for sails, sacks, canvas water hoses and fabrics as well as ropes. Today, hemp is primarily a niche crop in Europe with the main cultivator states being France, the United Kingdom and The Netherlands. European producers are utilizing hemp for a dizzying array of products to serve both European and U.S. markets. In fact, some sources suggest more than 25,000 products can be made from hemp with U.S. companies such as Ford Motors, Patagonia and The Body Shop having to import hemp materials from Canada, Europe and China. Hemp fibers are transformed into pulp that is largely

dedicated to the cigarette paper market while research financed by the European Commission and Member States has contributed to hemp entering into multiple other markets. For example, hemp fibers are used for insulation material, press and injection molding in the automotive industry, and mulch fleeces. Hemp uses in automobile manufacturing represents a growing market in Europe, with hemp bio-composites being utilized for door panels/inserts, trunk liners, spare wheel covers, parcel trays, and ABC pillars. In fact, in the early 20th century hemp cellulose was utilized for certain plastics with Henry Ford even building a prototype car from biocomposite materials that included hemp. Hemp shivs (the woody core fibers) also enjoy an important market in the region, with this material being the basis for high quality bedding material for horses and other animals. Hemp shivs are able to absorb moisture up to 4 times their dry weight while hemp bedding tends to rot down quickly into effective compost after use.

In addition, hemp shivs, in combination with lime, are increasingly being applied in construction. Hundreds of houses in France, UK and Ireland have been built with this material as well as in the building of a huge beer distribution warehouse and a major retail store. According to the European Industrial Hemp Association, this hemp based building material "is easy to handle, price competitive, shows good insulation properties for a construction material and it appears to be crack proof…. Eco-construction experts especially are seeing a great potential for Hemp-Lime Construction". Finally, hemp seeds and oil are competing in markets for animal feed, human food, and cosmetics. Though Canadian and Chinese producers are central actors in the market for Hemp seeds and oil, European producers harvested 6,000 metric tons of Hemp seeds in 2010. The fact that these seeds are an excellent source of important mineral nutrients and vitamins, balanced proteins and oil consisting of an impressive fatty acid spectrum is leading many European producers to view the food market as one with strong growth potential.

Renewable Resource and Sustainable Development

European producers and their interest groups are actively seeking to emphasize the centrality that Industrial Hemp can contribute to the EU's stated goals of reducing greenhouse emissions, while promoting renewable resources and sustainable development. Bio-based plastics and composites have witnessed a double-digit annual growth between 2008 and 2013 and are widely used in the European automotive industry—an industry in which hemp is already illustrating its potential in interior moldings. European researchers have found that hempfiber reinforced plastics demonstrate substantial energy and greenhouse gas savings in comparison to

their fossil-fuel competitors while hemp materials show great potential in replacing glass and mineral wool in insulation. Hemp can be grown in a variety of climates, is naturally resistant to pests and can be pulped with fewer chemicals than is used with wood.

Hemp producers have been lobbying the EU and member governments for greater subsidies and tariff protections in order to facilitate the expansion of Hemp production to improve the profitability of this valuable commodity relative to less environmentally and socially friendly competitors. John Hobson, President of the European Industrial Hemp Association, reported in the spring of 2015 that European Hemp Fibers would

soon be the first natural fiber worldwide with an established sustainability certification.

Industrial Hemp production in Europe has demonstrated the broad range of products and uses of Hemp. Market and scientific research has also illustrated the potential role that this commodity can contribute to the increasing need for economies throughout the world to integrate sustainable development and renewable resources in our global economy. The European model has also made clear, after decades of industrial scale production, that hemp can be produced without weakening laws regarding recreational cannabis and/or contributing to substance abuse.

Hemp seeds are an excellent source of protein.

Suggested readings:

Carus, Michael and Stefan Karst, Alexandre Kauffmann, John Hobson and Sylvestre Bertucelli. The European Hemp Industry: Cultivation, processing and applications for fibres, shivs and seeds, (The European Industrial Hemp Association, 2013). Available at http://eiha.org/media/2014/10/13-06-European-Hemp-Industry.pdf

European Industrial Hemp Association. Industrial Hemp in strong upturn, June 2015, Press Release. Available at http://eiha.org/media/2015/06/15-06-08-PR-EIHA-Conference.pdf

Johnson, Renée. "Hemp as an Agricultural Commodity". Congressional Research Service, 2015. Available at https://www.fas.org/sgp/crs/misc/RL32725.pdf

Luginbuhl, April M. Industrial Hemp (Cannabis savita L): The Geography of a Controversial Plant, California Geographer, vol. 41: 1-14, 2001).

Small, E. and D. Marcus. Hemp: A new crop with new uses for North America, p. 284–326. In: J. Janick and A. Whipkey (eds.), Trends in new crops and new uses. ASHS Press, Alexandria, VA., 2002) Available at https://www.hort.purdue.edu/newcrop/ncnu02/v5-284.html

Yonavjak, Logan. Industrial Hemp is a Win-Win for the Environment and Economy, Forbes, May 29th, 2014.

Hemp Derived CBD:
A New Frontier of Medicinal Uses

Karen Crocker

MS in Chemistry Retired Hospital Administrator

The medical community is witnessing a surge of research exploring the potential medicinal uses of hemp. New findings are already emerging, with early results indicating that Cannabidiol (CBD) based medicine shows real promise in addressing a number of serious conditions including seizures, systemic inflammation, and neurodegenerative disorders. Prior to delving into the chemical properties and the medicinal potential of hemp, it is important to ensure that there is a foundational understanding of the terminology.

Cannabis – A flowering plant that includes three species of the genus Cannabis: Cannabis ruderalis, Cannabis indica, and Cannabis sativa. Much of the confusion about marijuana and hemp is that they are both referred to as cannabis, which leads people to believe that they are one and the same. The International Association of Plant Taxonomy in 1976 concluded that "both hemp and marijuana varieties are of the same genus, Cannabis, and the same species, Cannabis Sativa." However, they are not "one and the same."

Marijuana – Cannabis with high levels of the psychoactive compound THC. The term marijuana is used when describing the Cannabis Sativa plant bred for its bulbous resin glands (known as trichomes) on the buds and flowers of the female plant. Trichomes contain high concentrations of THC. Historically, marijuana had one to five percent THC, but recent intense cultivation has dramatically increased THC levels.

Hemp – Low THC varieties of cannabis that are grown for fiber, oil, or seeds. The most common legal definition of hemp is that it has a THC level of 0.3 percent or less. Hemp strains were not developed to produce buds, and therefore lack the primary component (trichomes) that produce the marijuana high. By using selective breeding, growers have created hemp varieties with high levels of CBD and low levels of THC. It is impossible to get "high" by smoking or ingesting hemp, and it is also impossible to get high by consuming CBD oil products that contain no THC at all. The CBD in hemp actually has a mitigating effect on THC and dampen its psychoactive properties.

Cannabinoids – The 85 active chemical compounds present in cannabis. The preeminent cannabinoids are

Researchers are now actively evaluating hemp for medicinal purposes.

THC and CBD. The cannabinoids are a diverse chemical family that mimics the endocannabinoid chemicals naturally occurring in the human body. Endocannabinoids are critical to cell regulation - they work to maintain a stable internal cell environment in response to stress or injury. Different cannabinoids have widely varied effects, which scientists are just now beginning to study and understand.

Cannabidiol (CBD) – a naturally occurring cannabinoid and the second most abundant constituent of the Cannabis plant. CBD is legal and safe to consume, but is just now becoming the subject of serious scientific research to uncover its medicinal properties. It was thought by the general public to have psychoactive properties like THC, which is not true.

Tetrahydrocannabinol (THC) – A psychoactive cannabinoid, THC is responsible for the "high" from ingesting or inhaling marijuana. Because cannabinoid receptors are concentrated in areas of the brain associated with thinking, memory, pleasure, coordination and time perception, THC correspondingly affects all of those brain functions.

Medical use of cannabis has a lengthy history, dating back as far as 2900 BC when Emperor Fu of China recognized it for its medicinal properties. Prior to 1937, cannabis products were commonly used by U.S. physicians as accepted treatment. Public concern over marijuana

basically took all cannabis products out of the doctors' medicine bag in 1937. Fortunately, interest in cannabis is now undergoing a rebirth as a host of scientific studies are exploring its medicinal applications. Importantly, research is branching out from a nearlyexclusive focus on THC to an increasing interest in the CBD chemical properties which seem to hold particularly significant medicinal potential.

Chemical Profile

Both CBD and THC belong to a class of compounds known as cannabinoids.

THC

A THC molecule is composed of a combination of Carbon, Hydrogen, and Oxygen atoms. Its chemical formula is: $C_{21}H_{30}O_2$

THC stimulates parts of the brain causing the release of dopamine – creating a sense of euphoria, well-being and a sense of relaxation. These pathways, called CB1 receptors, are concentrated in the brain. THC also has analgesic effects, relieving the symptoms of pain and inflammation. Peak plasma levels of THC are normally achieved within 10 minutes of smoking marijuana. Intoxication lasts approximately two to three hours.

Because of its high lipid solubility, THC accumulates in fatty tissues, leading to its long half-life. Cannabinoids from marijuana used months ago can be detected in a urine drug screen because they are very slowly metabolized out of the body.

Despite all of the negative publicity due to its psychoactive properties, THC has desirable medical applications and is effective as a moderatestrength analgesic (a type of drug that offers relief from pain) and an effective form of treatment for the symptoms of diseases including HIVpositive individuals, and for cancer patients undergoing chemotherapy.

A CBD molecule is composed of a combination of Carbon, Hydrogen, and Oxygen atoms. Like THC, its chemical formula is: $C_{21}H_{30}O_2$
In biochemistry, the shape of molecules or the location of specific chemical groups (i.e. the -OH groups) affects which receptors on the surface of your cells they bind to, which leads to their differing effects.

CBD tends to be the second most abundant cannabinoid. It is a nonpsychoactive component that actually reduces and regulates the effects of THC. Even though both compounds have the same chemical formula, CBD is non-psychoactive because it does not act on the same cell surface receptor pathways as THC. CBD has a long list of potential medicinal uses, including the relief of conditions such as chronic pain, inflammation, migraines, arthritis, spasms, epilepsy and schizophrenia. CBD has also been shown to have anti-cancer properties.

Medical Properties of CBD

Medical Properties of CBD	Effects
Antiemetic	Reduces nausea and vomiting
Anticonvulsant	Suppresses seizure activity
Antipsychotic	Combats psychosis disorders
Antiinflammatory	Combats inflammatory disorders
Antioxidant	Combats neurodegenerative disorders
Antitumor/Anti-cancer	Combats tumor and cancer cells
Anxiolytic/Antidepressant	Combats anxiety and depression disorders

A 2011 review published in Current Drug Safety concludes that CBD does not interfere with psychomotor and psychological functions. The authors add that studies suggest that CBD is well tolerated and safe even at high doses. According to a 2013 review published in The British Journal of Clinical Pharmacology, studies have found CBD to possess the following medicinal properties:

Most of this evidence comes from animal models, since very few CBD studies have been carried out in human patients. A pharmaceutical version of CBD was recently developed by a drug company based in the UK. The company, GW Pharmaceuticals, is now funding clinical trials on CBD as a treatment for schizophrenia and certain types of epilepsy. A team of researchers at the California Pacific Medical Center, led by Dr. Sean McAllister, plan to begin trials on CBD as a breast cancer therapy.

A patent awarded to the U.S. Health and Human Services in 2003 (US6630507) covers the use of CBD as a treatment for various neurodegenerative and inflammatory disorders.

The following citations present a snapshot of the rich menu of ongoing CBD research. Note the very prestigious research institutions and journals that are involved with this research.

US 6630507 B1 (patent) Cannabinoids have been found to have antioxidant properties, unrelated to NMDA receptor antagonism. This new found property makes cannabinoids useful in the treatment and prophylaxis of wide variety of oxidation associated diseases, such as ischemic, agerelated, inflammatory and autoimmune diseases. The cannabinoids are found to have particular application as neuroprotectants, in limiting neurological damage following ischemic events, such as stroke and trauma, or in the treatment of neurodegenerative diseases, such as Alzheimer's disease, Parkinson's disease and HIV dementia. Nonpsychoactive cannabinoids, such as cannabidiol, are particularly advantageous to use because they avoid toxicity that is encountered with psychoactive cannabinoids at high doses useful in the method of the present invention.

Prevention of Alzheimer's Disease Pathology by Cannabinoids:
Neuroprotection Mediated by Blockade of Microglial Activation
Belén G. Ramírez, Cristina Blázquez, Teresa Gómez del Pulgar, Manuel Guzmán, and María L. de Cebala

The Journal of Neuroscience, 23 February 2005, 25(8): 19041913; doi: 10.1523/JNEUROSCI.454004.2005
The results indicate that cannabinoid receptors are important in the pathology of AD and that cannabinoids succeed in preventing the neurodegenerative process occurring in the disease.

Cannabidiol in Humans—The Quest for Therapeutic Targets
Pharmaceuticals (Basel). 2012 May; 5(5): 529–552.
Published online 2012 May 21.
Simon Zhornitsky and Stéphane Potvin
Cannabidiol (CBD) is attracting growing attention in medicine for its anxiolytic, antipsychotic, antiemetic and antiinflammatory properties. Ongoing research is determining whether cannabinoid ligands may be effective agents in the treatment of pain, glaucoma, the wasting and emesis associated with cancer chemotherapy and AIDS, and neurodegenerative disorders such as multiple sclerosis, epilepsy, spasms, anxiety disorders, bipolar disorder, schizophrenia, convulsions, and dementia.

One of the most promising areas is the ability of CBDs to affect a number of pathways involved in the cell survival/death decision.

Antitumor Effects of Cannabidiol, a Nonpsychoactive Cannabinoid, on Human Glioma Cell Lines

Stefania Ceruti, Arianna Colombo, Maria P. Abbracchio and Daniela Parolaro Department of Pharmacology, Chemotherapy and Toxicology (P.M., A.C.), and Department of Pharmacological Sciences, School of Pharmacy, and Center of Excellence for Neurodegenerative Diseases, University of Milan, Milan, Italy (S.C., M.P.A.); and Department of Structural and Functional Biology, Pharmacology Unit and Center of Neuroscience, University of Insubria, Busto Arsizio (Varese), Italy (A.V., D.P.)

The nonpsychoactive CBD was able to produce a significant antitumor activity both in vitro and in vivo, thus suggesting a possible application of CBD as an antineoplastic agent for glioblastomas.

Antitumor activity of plant cannabinoids with emphasis on the effect of cannabidiol on human breast carcinoma.

Ligresti A, Moriello AS, Starowicz K, Matias I, Pisanti S, De Petrocellis L, Laezza C, Portella G, Bifulco M, Di Marzo V.

Journal of Exp Pharm Ther: 2006

Both cannabidiol and the cannabidiolrich extract inhibited the growth of xenograft tumors. Our experiments indicate that cannabidiol effect is due to its capability of inducing apoptosis.

[9]Tetrahydrocannabinol inhibits epithelial growth factorinduced lung cancer cell migration in vitro as well as its growth and metastasis in vivo

A Preet, R K Ganju and J E Groopman Division of Experimental Medicine, Department of Medicine, Beth Israel Deaconess Medical Center, Harvard Medical School, Boston, MA, USA

Oncogene (2008) 27, 339–346; doi:10.1038/sj.onc.1210641; published online 9 July 2007

This study suggests that cannabinoids like THC should be explored as novel therapeutic molecules in controlling the growth and metastasis of certain lung cancers.

Antiproliferative and apoptotic effects of anandamide in human prostatic cancer cell lines: implication of epidermal growth factor receptor downregulation and ceramide production (2003)

National Library of Medicine

This research outlines how the activation of cannabinoid receptors within the prostate causes antiprolific effect in cancer cells, having large implications into the treatment of prostate cancer.

Tetrahydrocannabinolinduced apoptosis in Jurkat leukemia T cells is regulated by translocation of Bad to mitochondria (2006)

National Library of Medicine

This Research outlines the assessment of the use of cannabinoids to cause apoptosis (the regulated and natural death of cells). It gained positive results, finding that cannabinoids do indeed cause the death of cancerous leukemia cells.

Expression of cannabinoid receptors type 1 and type 2 in nonHodgkin lymphoma: Growth inhibition by receptor activation (2008)

International Journal of Cancer

This research was conducted to determine what the effects of cannabinoid receptor activation on lymphoma were. It was found that cannabinoid receptor activation reduced the multiplication and growth of lymphoma, as well as causing some cancer cells to die.

The role of cannabinoids in prostate cancer: Basic science perspective and potential clinical applications (2012)

National Library of Medicine

This research concluded that it would be in everyone's best interest to conduct human clinical trials involving medical cannabis.

NonTHC cannabinoids inhibit prostate carcinoma growth in vitro and in vivo: proapoptotic effects and underlying mechanisms (2013)

National Library of Medicine

This research set out to expand on the previously researched notion that cannabinoid receptor activation caused cell death within prostate cancer cells. The research found significant positive results and concluded that the data supported the clinical testing of CBD in prostate cancer patients.

Cannabinoid ReceptorMediated Apoptosis Induced by R(+) Methanandamide and Win55,2122 Is Associated with Ceramide Accumulation and p38 Activation in Mantle Cell Lymphoma (2006)

Molecular Pharmacology

This study set out to explore whether cannabinoids inhibited cancer cells in lymphoma. It outlines how cannabinoids were found to cause growth inhibition and cell death within mantle cell lymphoma (blood cancer).

Cannabinoids inhibit cellular respiration of human oral cancer cells (2010)

National Library of Medicine

This research aimed to study the effects of cannabinoids on how cancerous cells respire within types of oral cancer. They found that cannabinoids inhibit the cancer cells respiration and are thus toxic to them. This implies that cannabinoids could be used for the treatment of oral cancer.

Antitumor action of cannabinoids on hepatocellular carcinoma: role of AMPK-dependent activation of autophagy (2011)

National Library of Medicine

This research aimed to determine how THC affects cancerous cells within the liver. It was found that THC reduces the growth and effectiveness of the cancerous cell, implying that CBD as a therapeutic treatment should be explored further.

Cannabinoids Induce Apoptosis of Pancreatic Tumor Cells via Endoplasmic Reticulum Stress–Related Genes (2006)

American Journal of Cancer

The study found that when cannabinoids were administered, cancer cells started dying through apoptosis, leading to a reduction in tumor growth and its spread.

Anecdotal evidence for the use of CBD-Derived Medicine

Perhaps one of the most startling breakthroughs with CBD is its ability to effectively treat seizure disorders. Dravet Syndrome is an extremely debilitating form of seizure disorder in children. Victims are plagued by seizures, often up to hundreds a day. Cannabidiol appears to have the capability to treat Dravet Syndrome. One success story involves a 5-year-old girl named Charlotte who suffered with 300 seizures per week. She was given a tincture version of CBD taken from a cannabis strain that was specifically

developed to provide her with the benefits of the drug without the psychoactive THC. After treatment, seizure frequency dropped dramatically to 23 per month. This story received wide national exposure, including a report by Dr. Sanjay Gupta, Chief Medical Correspondent for CNN.

A second episode involving CBD and Dravet Syndrome occurred in 2011. Jason David teamed up with Harborside Health Center to create a cannabisbased treatment for his son Jayden, who suffered from dozens of seizures per day. Their groundwork made it possible for companies like CW Botanicals, the producers of the Charlotte's tincture of hemp oil, to develop their product for patient use. The story of the Davids and Harborside Health Center was featured in the six-episode Discovery Channel show Weed Wars.

These two anecdotes are not unique. Stanford researchers found that of 19 severely epileptic children given CBD-enriched cannabis, 84% experienced substantial seizure reduction. A limited number of patients are now receiving an orally-administered liquid containing CBD under the brand name Epidiolex, which received orphan drug status in the U.S. for use as a treatment for Dravet syndrome.

CBD has no lethal dose or known serious medical side effects, traits which create a prime opportunity for the development of a variety of CBD-derived medicines. The FDA seems to agree,

recently approving a study to examine the effects of CBD on epilepsy, specifically in young users. Commercially available cannabinoids, such as dronabinol and nabilone, are approved drugs for the treatment of cancer-related side effects. Nabiximols (Sativex), a Cannabis extract with a 1:1 ratio of THC:CBD, is approved in Canada (under the Notice of Compliance with Conditions) for symptomatic relief of pain in advanced cancer and multiple sclerosis. Canada, New Zealand, and some countries in

Europe also approved nabiximols for spasticity of multiple sclerosis, a common symptom that may include muscle stiffness, reduced mobility, and pain, for which existing therapy is unsatisfactory.

CBD is becoming the drug of choice in the research world because it promises relief from many different diseases and conditions. Several states have passed what are known as CBD oil laws, which allow qualifying patients to avoid prosecution for possessing cannabis oil.

Hemp Use In Veterinary Medicine

ALLISON JENKINS, DVM

OWNER, HIGHLAND ANIMAL CLINIC DENVER COLORADO

More than 50 percent of Americans share their homes with a dog or cat. As most pet owners know, animals can affect us in countless positive ways, on many different levels. Pets have the ability to decrease stress, enhance mood, and boost immunity. The Centers for Disease Control and the National Institute of Health conducted a variety studies that consistently find pet owners exhibit decreased blood pressure, cholesterol, and triglyceride levels, therefore potentially decreasing their risk for having a heart attack. Studies have also shown that pet owners tend to have higher levels of the neurotransmitters serotonin and dopamine, which have pleasurable, calming, and relaxing effects on our body and psyche. Additional health benefits of pets include increased activity and exercise, as most pets encourage us to get outside and play. Pets can also help on the social front, encouraging human interaction and giving us something to talk about. They are great conversation pieces and ease anxiety. Pets have the ability to act as teachers to young and old alike, by fostering responsibility, kindness, and patience. Dogs and cats provide us with love and laughter. To many, they are our best friends.

The human-animal bond is strengthening every day, as evidenced by the ever-growing pet industry. It is estimated that Americans spent over $60 billion on their pets last year, and that number is growing annually. A good portion of sales, approximately 25 percent, is spent on keeping our pets healthy through veterinary medicine. Pets experience many of the same ailments as their owners, including, but not limited to: seizures, arthritis, and anxiety. Veterinarians and pet owners alike are constantly searching for innovative ways to help their best friends cope with these common illnesses. Interestingly enough, hemp is showing that it has the potential

Americans spend $15 billion per year keeping our pets healthy.

to help, and even potentially heal, some of our animals with serious health issues.

Anyone who has ever had a pet that suffered from seizures knows the helpless feeling that comes with the condition. Minutes feels like hours and you just want relief for your pet. Epilepsy is the recurrence of seizures over weeks to months and is the most common chronic neurologic disorder of dogs. It affects upwards of 5.7 percent of dogs, and often proves difficult to manage. In patients one to five years old, there is often no discernible cause for epilepsy and treatment is strictly symptomatic, aimed at controlling the frequency and duration of the seizures. Seizures can lead to brain damage and, in patients that continue to seize despite treatment, humane euthanasia may be considered.

Traditional seizure medications, called antiepileptics, can cause many undesirable side effects, such as sedation, liver toxicity, and hind limb weakness. Patients often experience increased thirst and hunger, along with behavioral changes. These antiepileptic drugs may help to decrease seizure activity, but the negative effects often diminish the patient's quality of life. It is not uncommon to require multiple drugs to control a patient's seizures, adding to the potential for serious side effects. It is also necessary to monitor the drug levels and liver enzymes of patients receiving antiepileptics. The combination of drugs and monitoring can become quite expensive.

Degenerative joint disease, commonly called arthritis, is a degenerative, progressive and irreversible disease process of joints. An estimated one in five adult dogs suffers from arthritis. This equates to 10–12 million dogs in the US showing signs of arthritis! Dogs demonstrate their pain from arthritis in varying degrees. It often first appears as a reluctance to perform common tasks and activities, such as going up the stairs or jumping in the car. It may then progress to lack of mobility, decreased muscle tone, and obvious lameness. Arthritis is one of the most common causes of chronic pain in our canine patients. In older, largebreed dogs, it is also one of the most common reasons for humane euthanasia. No one wants their best friend in pain.

Degenerative joint disorders are probably as common in cats as in dogs, but cats are less likely to exhibit overt clinical signs such as lameness. Studies have shown that as many as 90 percent of cats older than 12 had radiographic evidence of arthritis. Common feline symptoms of arthritis include grooming difficulties, inappropriate urination and defecation, less jumping, aggressiveness when handled, and lameness. It is a silent disease that likely affects many of our older feline patients.

There is no cure for arthritis, so treatment is aimed at control. The most effective approach is multimodal directed at protecting the joints, increasing mobility, and most importantly, controlling pain. It is a multibillion dollar industry and for good reason. Humans can relate to the negative effects of arthritis and want to help their pets as much as possible. So, pet owners buy the joint supplements, the fish oil, and try different pain medications, in hopes of improving their pet's quality of life.

Arthritis is especially frustrating because it is progressive and many of the pain medications come with undesirable side effects, risks, and costs. Pain medications, such as opioids, can help control a patient's pain, but often cause sedation and constipation. Nonsteroidal antiinflammatories (NSAID's), although often highly effective, come with the risk of gastric ulcers or potential liver damage. And cats can't tolerate NSAID's for more than a few days, so their choices for pain relief are even more limited!

Another ailment that we share with our pets is anxiety. It is more commonly recognized and treated today than ever before. Anxiety may be the result of breeding, environment, or both. It can affect whether or not a rescued animal stays in their adoptive home and how much interaction a pet gets with other animals and people. Mental disease

in our pets, as in humans, is real and deserves attention.

In cases where pets may be surrendered or their anxiety is affecting their everyday life, antianxiety medications, such as Prozac or Xanax may be considered. These medications have the potential for side effects such as sedation, personality, and behavior changes. These side effects are probably less appreciated in our pets because they are unable to verbalize how they are feeling to us.

Our pets suffer from many of the same ailments and disease processes as we do. They also experience many of the same undesirable side effects to the medications we use. We must consider alternative, effective treatments to improve our pets' quality of life. A very exciting, emerging treatment that we fortunately have at our

disposal is hemp. It is a unique treatment option, as it has proven to be effective with minimal, if any, side effects. Hemp must be considered, explored, and used where appropriate in veterinary medicine.

Veterinarian science is just now beginning to explore the impact of hempbased treatments, so there are still unanswered questions. Hemp primarily contains CBD, which is not psychoactive like the THC in marijuana, but has antispasmodic, antiinflammatory, analgesic, antianxiety and antioxidant properties. CBD also has been shown to decrease nausea, increase appetite, and has the potential to cause cancer cell death. Pets, like humans, have an Endocannabinoids System (ECS) and cannabidiol receptors throughout various organs in their bodies, just waiting to be filled and activated by CBD so that its effects can be realized. There are many different forms of CBD-type products out there, from topical lotions and tinctures to oral capsules and treats. There is an advantage to using the entire hemp plant for medicinal purposes in pets, instead of CBD-only products. The hemp plant contains multiple components, such as the abovementioned CBD, as well as other phytocannabinoids, terpenes and flavonoids. The terpenes act to modulate the cannabinoids, while the flavonoids act as potentantiinflammatories. There are also several essential fatty acids and vitamins present in hemp. Additionally, the low level of THC found in hemp is necessary in specific ratios with CBD to

make it effective.

Much of the research regarding the medicinal properties of hemp for pets has been extrapolated from human data, given our shared Endocannabinoids Systems. Veterinarians have been and are currently researching hemp's effects, both in clinical and scientific settings. Owners have been experimenting with it on their own pets, especially when traditional medicine has been ineffective or their pets have been diagnosed with a terminal condition. The results have been encouraging and, in some cases miraculous, for our beloved pets.

The neuroprotective and anticonvulsive properties of cannabidiol has been extensively studied and is currently a very hot topic in the human research field. In veterinary clinical studies, uncontrolled seizure patients have gained control with hemp and others have been able to decrease or eliminate other traditional medications when adding in hemp. This is very exciting news, as it has always been a big decision to start a pet on antiepileptics due to their likelihood of causing sedation and weakness. We, as veterinarians, now have an alternative that actually works to protect the nervous system, while potentially decreasing seizures.

Perhaps the most common use for hemp today is to treat pain from arthritis. It can be used as an adjunct with other treatments or alone when owners first notice differences in their pet's activity level. Cannabinoids are effective at controlling both chronic and acute pain by modulating pain signals in the nervous system and exhibiting an antiinflammatory effect. There is also no need to monitor liver values or worry about gastric ulceration when using hemp products. Results by veterinarians conducting their own clinical trials have been very promising and most have seen notable improvements in their patients suffering from arthritis. Additionally, cats can take hemp just like dogs!

Hemp is also currently being used for pets with anxiety. Animals suffering from separation anxiety, sleep disorders, and cognitive dysfunction have seen calming, not sedative, effects with the use of hemp. It can also be used in conjunction with other traditional medications or alone.

The most common side effects seen with administration of hemp in pets are mild diarrhea or lethargy, which are usually selflimiting within a few days. Rarely, vomiting or skin sensitivity may occur, in which case the hemp should be discontinued. These side effects are few and far between, with the vast majority of patients seeing improvement of their conditions over days to weeks. Most patients have continued on the hemp longterm because of the positive effects on their quality of life.

There is exciting work to be done on cannabinoids and their effects on cancer. We know that cancerous tissues express higher numbers of cannabinoid receptors than noncancerous tissues. Binding of those receptors has been shown to cause cancer cell death. In addition, CBD has been shown to be antinausea and appetitestimulating, both of which are issues in patients suffering from different forms of cancer.

Hemp has real potential to improve our pets' quality of life. As evidenced by the positive clinical studies and American pet owners' willingness to properly care for their pets, it is an area that demands attention and research, both on an individual and group level. Pets do so much for us every day, by giving us unconditional love and constant companionship. Don't we owe them the research and effort to find if access to hempbased treatments can give them longer, happier lives?

Twelve foot tall naturally occurring hemp in south-central Nebraska

Agricultural Commodities as Fuel

Jacob Borden, PhD

Assistant Professor Department of Chemical, Civil, and Mechanical Engineering McNeese State University

The use of crops to produce fuel and energy dates to before the turn of the 20th century, garnering significant attention in the earliest days of what was, at the time, the latest and greatest technology – the internal combustion engine. There was no simple process to produce the high-quality liquid fuels necessary for these new engines, which had narrow operating tolerances relative to boiler-powered steam engines. Petroleum refiners such as Standard Oil produced large volumes of highly variable grades of kerosene and naptha, which are similar but not the same as modern diesel and gasoline. By comparison, the production of relatively pure vegetable oils and ethanol for heating, lighting, cooking and even drinking was already well-developed, with both products being ubiquitous and sold in high volumes. It was only natural that the internal combustion engine pioneers would consider crop-based fuels during the earliest days of development.

Over time the cost, quality and availability of petroleum-based fuels improved dramatically, and fuels from agricultural commodities were relegated to limited and specialized applications. For instance, Prohibition-era bootleggers understood that ethanol improved octane when mixed with gasoline, allowing them to tune their engines to operate at an increased combustion pressure, thus improving power and top speed. Likewise methanol and ethanol are sometimes used in Formula One racing fuels. In addition to increasing the octane of gasoline, the oxygen atom found in each ethanol molecule improves fuel combustion and thereby reduces tailpipe emissions of unburned hydrocarbons. As for vegetable oils, some drivers in Europe still respond to high fuel taxes by mixing a few liters of the European equivalent of canola oil with their petrol.

The ongoing advances in biotechnology and improvements in agricultural practices since 1960 have combined to increase the yield from each acre planted, thereby reducing the cost of producing fuels from commodity crops. Yield improvements are particularly striking in corn and soybeans. Data from the USDA indicates that the number of bushels of corn harvested per acre has increased almost linearly from about 60 bushels per acre in 1960 to 135

The U.S. produced more than 1.26 billion gallons of biodiesel in 2015

Hemp can yield 9 tons of dry fiber per acre.

bushels in 2000. By 2014, average yields had improved further, to an impressive 165 bushels per year. Peak yields have increased just as dramatically. Every year the National Corn Growers Association holds a cornyield competition, with the 2014 contest winner setting an alltime record by harvesting 503 bushels of corn from a single acre. The yield of soybeans has nearly doubled, increasing from 25 bushels per acre in 1960 to 48 in 2015. Additionally, varietal selection and improved growing practices have increased the oil content of soybeans from 35% to 45% of the seed. The economics of commodity crop production had thereby improved such that, as early as

2004, the price of corn and the price of oil reached parity when compared on the basis of energy content.

Improved agricultural productivity has coincided with advances in biotechnology that now deliver designer enzymes and organisms genetically tailored to successfully convert an everwidening variety of complex biomass. The sugars in starch are easy to break down with enzymes compared to the sugars in grasses and woody biomass, which are locked in a more complex matrix of three polymers collectively termed "lignocellulose." While relatively moderate temperatures and simple enzymes, such as the ones in your saliva, are sufficient to break down starch,

the conditions and chemicals necessary to decompose lignocellulose to sugars are severe enough to generate byproducts that are toxic to fermenting organisms. The initial clue for the solution to the problem came from an unexpected source the canvas tents used by American troops in Vietnam in the 1960s. When these tents began to rot, it was discovered that a fungus that produced enzymes capable of breaking down the cellulose in the canvas was the culprit. This cellulose is also the major component of lignocellulose. The intervening decades have seen gradual improvement in the enzyme cocktails and processing techniques that yield a maximum amount of fermentable sugars from lignocellulose.

Incremental advances in technologies that underpin crop-based fuel and energy production have improved the economic potential of using grasses, wood and other biomass as feedstock. In addition, renewable fuels legislation enacted in 2005 and expanded in 2007 introduced mandates for fuels produced from traditional crops as well as from lignocellulosic biomass. The mandate created significant investment in assets and technologies for producing ethanol and more advanced fuels from biomass. In 2007, the U.S. produced 6.5 billion gallons of ethanol, only slightly more ethanol than Brazil produced. By 2014, upwards of $50 billion had been invested just in corn-ethanol production capacity to meet mandated blending levels. U.S. ethanol production increased to over

14 billion gallons in 2014, while Brazil still produced just over 6 billion gallons. Technological advance continues in 2015, POET, a South Dakota based biofuels company, commissioned the world's first commercial-scale facility for the production of ethanol from corn stover — the stalks, leaves and cobs of the corn plant.

The ability to convert an even larger fraction of the entire corn plant has stimulated interest in evaluating other nontraditional sources of biomass. Research programs across the globe are investigating the fuel potential of alternative crops, including the jerusalem artichoke, sugar beets, sweet sorghum, switchgrass, sugar cane and, of course, hemp.

Plant-Based Fuel Technology

Like other such crops, the complex botany of hemp can be simplified into two important components – stalks and seeds. Hemp leaves contribute a relatively minor amount to the overall yield of harvested biomass. Stalks and seeds themselves contain different amounts of those molecules with potential as sources of fuels and chemicals – proteins, hemp oil and lignocellulose, the last being more commonly known as fiber. While the stalks are principally made of fiber, the seeds contain roughly equal amounts of fiber, oil and proteins.

Technologies exist today for the conversion of both stalks and seeds to fuels. Hemp oil can be readily separated

Existing technology can convert hemp stalk to fuel.
Photo by Alf Riberio/Shutterstock.com

Agricultural Commodities as Fuel | 115

from the fiber and proteins in hemp seeds, using the same processes long employed to extract oils from legumes such as canola and soybeans. The fiber and protein portion of seeds are often ground to form an animal meal, and hempbased meals provide nutritional value in the diets of ruminants, chickens, and pigs (1, 2, 3). In corn-ethanol production, 30-35% of each kernel is protein and other soluble but inert compounds that are dried and sold as Dried Distiller's Grains, or DDGs. Meanwhile hemp produces seeds with about 30% oil, compared to 40-45% for today's relatively well-optimized soybeans.

Hemp oils are relatively lower in saturated fats than soybean oil, which provides for reduced viscosity and cloud point - the cold temperature at which the oil begins to gel (4). These properties make hemp oil more amenable for use directly in diesel engines year-round, as opposed to those oils that must be modified to compensate for the increased viscosity of vegetable oil relative to diesel fuel. Otherwise, hemp and other oils themselves can be modified to reduce viscosity, such as by reacting the oil with methanol to produce biodiesel. Most recently, refinerybased catalysts have been developed that convert plant oils into fuel with a nearidentical chemical fingerprint to that of diesel fuel.

The lignocellulosic fibers in stalks and leaves are more chemically complex than seed oil, requiring multiple conversion steps using relatively severe treatment conditions to produce fuel. The principle method for producing fuel from stalks begins like the production of paper, with chemicals, steam or some combination of the two weakening the stalk fiber. Of the three polymers that make up each fiber, two are based on sugars that can be depolymerized, called cellulose and hemicellulose. The nonsugar polymer, or lignin, is more chemically inert than the two sugar polymers and is often burned for fuel once the sugar polymers have been decomposed. The types of chemicals and the severity with which the fibers are treated and pulped dictates the decomposition of one, two, or all three polymer fractions, although in most cases all three fractions are decomposed to varying degrees.

Depolymerization of the sugar polymers all the way to monomers is absolutely necessary for microbial fermentation, but the sugars themselves are also highly reactive and, once produced, will quickly degrade to relatively toxic by-products. To limit toxin production, treatment severity is often reduced, leaving the cellulose and hemicellulose relatively more intact. Fortunately these relatively more mild treatments still weaken and disrupt the fiber structures sufficiently that specialized enzymes, such as the ones isolated during Vietnam, are able to complete the depolymerization and form fermentable sugars.

The bacteria and yeast used in fermentation are likewise heavily genetically engineered for improved capability. For instance, much like

children behave in the presence of vegetables, microbes will ignore the sugar from hemicellulose in favor of cellulosic sugar. Genetic modifications have therefore been introduced that coax these microbes to consume both sugars. Another trait being introduced is tolerance – tolerance to ethanol, which is itself toxic, as well as the toxic byproducts formed during treatment of the stalks. Also, because ethanol as an additive in fuel has significant drawbacks, fermentation microbes are also being engineered to produce molecules with improved fuel characteristics. Microbes now exist that produce good proxies of the chemical fingerprints and fuel characteristics of gasoline and diesel.

A second principle method for generating fuel from fibrous stalks involves partial-combustion of the stalks at temperatures in excess of 900° Fahrenheit. The result is a combination of small, reactive gases (principally carbon monoxide and hydrogen) collectively referred to as syngas. Syngas is then passed over a catalyst, causing the small reactive gases to combine into a distribution of hydrocarbons similar to diesel fuel. However the high operating temperatures combined with expensive precious-metal catalysts have precluded biomass-based syngas production from commercialization.

In short, the pathways available to convert plants to fuels and chemicals can be applied to the conversion of hemp. Although some treatment conditions

The three drivers of crop-based fuels production are the yield of harvested biomass, the "capital intensity" of the conversion process, and the conversion yield from biomass to the final fuel(s). Of these three, the parameter with the greatest influence on the overall cost of the fuel is the dry tons of biomass – stalks and seeds – harvested per acre planted. This is of such importance because many other logistical and production factors depend on it. Foremost, a lower yield of dry tons means proportionally more acreage must be dedicated to supply a processing facility. More acres planted also means more fuel and fertilizer will be needed. As the required acreage increases, so too does average hauling distance, and therefore freight cost from the field to the facility gate.

As mentioned earlier, corn yields have been averaging 165 bushels, 60-70% of which is starch that can be converted to ethanol with the rest being sold as animal feed. The yield of corn stover is about the same as for the kernels – 165 bushels equals about 4.3 tons of stalks and cobs – of which 20-30% must be left to replenish and protect the soil over winter. Currently all the corn stover is left in the field, with the exception of the state-of-the-art POET facility in Emmetsburg, Iowa. The corn kernel also contains a small amount of corn oil, however it is only recovered as a separate product in facilities that separate the kernel into multiple food staples such as corn meal, bran, gluten and flour.

have been tested on hemp, the range of chemicals and treatment severities has not been exhausted for this potential feedstock, let alone optimized. Research groups, mostly in Europe, have tested the conversion of hemp stems with a handful of chemicals – pressurized hot water, oxygen-impregnated hot water, high-temperature steam, ammonia, and dilute acids and bases. The majority of the available reports have focused on treating hemp with dilute sulfuric acid, because sulfuric acid is generally effective at treating many types of lignocellulose and therefore serves as a good baseline for comparing the conversion and economic potential among feedstock alternatives.

Economic Drivers of Biomass Based Fuels

Regardless of the methods employed for conversion, the economics of producing fuels from any crop begins by estimating three core parameters that drive the price of the finished fuel. An appreciation for the nature and relative magnitudes of these three parameters also allows for a simplified model whereby alternative pathways to the same fuel can be compared on a common basis. For this comparison, U.S. corn-based ethanol represents a mature industry whose cost and profit structures are known, and is therefore a reasonable selection with which to compare the feasibility of hempbased biofuels and energy.

Studies on the growth and productivity of hemp indicate that certain varieties and growth conditions favor the production of either stems or seeds. In general, the research literature on hemp cultivation supports yield estimates of 5 to 9 tons of hemp fiber per acre (5,6). For seed production the yields range between one-quarter and one-half of a ton per acre (5,6). The composition of the fibers are consistent to that of corn stover and other types of lignocellulose between 50-60% cellulose, 15% each of lignin and hemicellulose, and 10% other biological compounds including oils, waxes, and minerals.

Considering the range of biomass yields cited above - and conversion yields to be discussed shortly - the cultivation of hemp to produce ethanol would require roughly the same number of acres as making ethanol from corn. At 10 tons per acre, hemp would require about 35% fewer acres, while at 5 tons per acre hemp would require about 30% more. Fertilizer consumption would also be inline with current practices for growing corn, ranging from 50-150 pounds of nitrogen per acre (6,7).

The other two economic parameters are capital intensity and conversion yield. Capital intensity refers to the cost to install one gallon of annual production capacity, and is related to the conversion yield. Both contribute to how large and expensive the equipment must be for a certain annual production rate. Obviously the capital intensity for a process increases

directly as the cost of the processing equipment itself increases. Meanwhile, the conversion yield determines how much biomass must be processed to generate a fixed number of gallons, or alternatively, how many gallons of final product are produced to distribute the capital costs from a fixed tonnage of feed.

For estimation, the capital intensity of operating facilities will often fall within a certain range based on the type of processing involved. For instance, refinery and petrochemical operations typically

require a capital intensity of between $1 and $3, meaning that an average-sized refinery producing 2 billion gallons of fuel per year would have an installed-cost of between $2 and $6 billion dollars. Handling and processing solids – such as milling corn and expressing the oil from soybeans – necessarily requires equipment that is more robust, less scalable and therefore more expensive. Such processes may have capital intensities as low as $3-$5 per gallon, or as high $10 - $20 for those processes that also require elevated

Hemp researchers are developing strains which will maximize biofuel production

temperatures, corrosive chemicals, or both. The most expensive industries are usually those where process and product standards are most strict – equipment for large-scale preparation of foods and especially pharmaceuticals, for instance.

The capital intensity of commercial-scale facilities for producing ethanol from corn ranges around $4 - 6 per gallon of annual ethanol production capacity. However, the fibrous nature of lignocellulose requires relatively harsher conditions acids at elevated temperatures which in turn means that the process equipment will require more specialized and expensive metallurgy. The installed cost of high-alloy piping and process equipment can be 24 times that of standard 304-type stainless steels. As a result, the impact is to double the capital intensity of traditional corn-ethanol milling.

In addition, lignocellulose is inherently more resistant to depolymerization than starch, which is a metabolic storage molecule specifically tailored through evolution to break down easily with enzymes. Lignocellulose serves as the structural support of the plant, which also makes it much more inert. The three-polymer, insoluble matrix that comprises lignocellulose also means that multiple types of enzymes in solution have to interact with a solid surface, whereas starch can partially dissolve in water and therefore react directly. These significant barriers to conversion mean that ethanol production from hemp will require relatively large and expensive processing equipment, and will require relatively more hemp per gallon of ethanol produced.

Conservative estimates for corn processing are that 95% of the available starch can be converted to sugars, and that the yield of ethanol by yeast fermentation is 95% of the maximum possible. Meanwhile, yields of sugar from both cellulose and hemicellulose from hemp are in the range of 60-80% (8,9). Fermentation yields from these two types of sugar are also lower than for starch, and also on the order of 60-80% of the maximum possible (9). Overall, every ton of processed corn yields about 120 gallons of ethanol, while every ton of hemp would yield closer to 50, at most 90 gallons. Taken together an approximate doubling of the cost of processing equipment and conversion yields of onehalf that for cornbased ethanol, it is easy to see why estimates of the capital intensity of biomassbased fuels might exceed $15 or $20 per gallon.

Of course, there are other factors of importance to the overall economics, such as the production of coproduct oils and animal feeds, the cost of digestion enzymes, logistics and other freight charges, as well as natural gas and electricity useage. However these are certainly less important than the three already mentioned. More important for this comparison, variations in these factors are relatively small between corn-based and hemp-based ethanol production.

The principal economic factor driving investment in biomassbased fuels production remains the availability of tax incentives and subsidies at both the state and federal levels. For example, multiple state and federal programs provide loan guarantees that reduce interest rates and therefore subsidize the significant upfront investment required for conversion facilities. Also, significant non-operational revenues can be realized due to a subsidy in the form of a mandate on oil refiners to purchase renewable fuel credits, called RIN's. Every gallon of biomassbased fuel generates a certain number of credits. In the case of corn-ethanol, one gallon of ethanol corresponds to one RIN credit. Fuels made from lignocellulose generate even more credits - upwards of 3 per gallon.

Each year the EPA certifies the number of credits that refiners must purchase, either by producing ethanol directly or by purchasing RIN credits from other parties. While the value of a RIN fluctuates with anticipated near-term demand for fuel and production of ethanol, the average price of one credit has held relatively steady at about $0.50. Considering a facility that produces 100 million gallons of ethanol, credit-based revenues could add $50 million to the bottom line of a corn-ethanol mill, and upwards of $150 million for a facility producing ethanol from hemp. Of course the impact of these interventions on market structure is significant. As mentioned above, $50 billion has been invested to double U.S. capacity to produce ethanol from corn, and billions more has been invested by companies and the government alike to foster the development of 2nd generation lignocellulosic technology.

Profitability of Corn and Hemp-Based Fuels

With an appreciation for the major economic factors of production, an estimate can be made for the value of dedicating scarce acreage and investment capital to the production of fuels from any crop. The cornethanol industry serves as a useful benchmark because it has relatively well-established operating performances and capital cost structures. To that end, the corn-ethanol yield and capital intensity figures cited previously can be combined with current (April, 2016) spot prices for corn ($3.50 per bushel), ethanol ($1.50 per gallon) and

dried-distillers grains ($175 per ton), as well as industry-average cost estimates for enzymes, maintenance, personnel and overhead.

For hemp, the three significant economic parameters are subject to much greater uncertainty, which necessitates evaluating across the potential ranges. Further, there is an additional economic constraint that must be applied to the cultivation of an alternative crop such as hemp. That is, each acre dedicated to one crop forgoes the potential revenue from planting the nearest alternative. Therefore the set of possible hemp performance parameters that are economically competitive must be constrained to those that result in the equivalent peracre return as for corn.

The impact of taxes is certainly germane to the nearterm economic potential of hemp and other biomass alternatives. For this comparison, the impact of taxes and subsidies are taken as follows:

Every gallon of cornethanol receives one RIN credit, while one gallon of hempethanol receives three RIN credits, with RIN credits valued at $0.50.

State and federal loan guarantees reduce the cost of capital to that of the 20-year federal treasury bond rate.

The 20 year MACRS depreciation schedule reduces taxable income over a 20-yr investment horizon.

A combined state federal corporate income tax rate of 40% applies to taxable income.

Table 1: Profitability and performance comparison for a facility producing 100 million gallons of ethanol per year from either corn or hemp. The row "Feedstock Price" represents the spot price for corn, but for hemp the row represents the hemp price that generates equivalent revenue per acre as with corn. IRR* represents the return excluding revenues from RIN credits.

Assumed values and economic results are available in Table 1 for producing ethanol from both corn and hemp. As mentioned, dedicating acreage to crops is an exercise in maximizing profitability per acre. Therefore, as the assumed yield of hemp drops, the required feedstock price must rise. If the costs of cultivation and harvesting are comparable between corn and hemp more on that later then revenue alone suffices as a basis for breakeven profitability, or $600 per acre for corn.

At a capital intensity of $5 per gallon for corn-ethanol, a facility producing 100 million gallons annually would cost about $500 million dollars to construct and generate $250 million in total annual revenues, 20% of which is derived from the sale of RIN credits. The result is a positive return of 10-11%. Returns climb to 20% if the capital intensity is instead assumed to be on the order of $3 per gallon, but drop to near-zero in the absence of revenues from the sale of RIN's.

The best-case scenario for the production of hemp involves harvesting 10 tons of fiber and 0.5 tons of seeds per acre, 80% yields for both the sugar production and yeast fermentation steps, and a capital intensity on the order of $10 per gallon. At these relatively optimistic

conditions, and including the sale of three RIN credits for every gallon produced, the economics of producing ethanol from hemp at least equals the economics of making it from corn. Under this scenario the conversion facility provides returns in excess of the expected cost of capital, which is itself reduced by the state and federal loan guarantees mentioned previously. The return remains positive even for the midpoint performance case, however a negative return is realized under the most pessimistic set of assumptions. In all cases, negative returns are realized without the assistance of RIN revenues which, at three credits per gallon, exceed those from the sale of ethanol.

Conclusions & Observations

Each of the scenarios considered above provide equal revenue to the farmer. However the cost of cultivating and harvesting hemp are not necessarily the same as for corn. Because hemp stalks don't pack together as compactly as seeds, each truck payload provides less biomass as compared with an equivalent volume of seeds or corn kernels. Stalks will therefore incur a higher transport cost per ton of biomass delivered.

Compared with the advanced agronomic practices that continue to propel corn yields, relatively little is known about the regularity of hemp yields relative to soil quality and nutrient availability. This limits our knowledge not only about the potential cost of cultivating hemp, but of hemp's maximum potential yield. Reported yields

The major advantage for hemp-based biofuels over other novel feedstocks is the fact that there are multiple enduses for it's products - hemp fibers in paper and textiles and oils in foods and nutraceuticals, for instance. Like in sugarcane production, the fiber from hemp can always be burned to generate steam and electricity, or pelletized and sold for use in biomass boilers. Farmers are more likely to take up a crop that has multiple and sustainable product outlets.

of hemp fiber per acre are at best half that for such prolific grasses as switchgrass or energy cane, a high-fiber variety of sugarcane, with yields approaching 25-30 dry tons per acre.

Hemp does have a very distinct advantage over these other grasses, in that hemp produces oil-bearing seeds. This provides both co-product revenues and product diversification, and hemp oils also may find higher value as nutraceuticals and food additives. While diesel at $2 per gallon is equivalent to $0.25 per pound, soybean oil sells for closer to $0.35 per pound.

Seed formation is also an important factor in cultivation practices. Grasses that don't form seeds reproduce by forming buds at the nodes of parent stalks, where one acre of parent stalks will seed about 10-15 acres. The parent stalks have to be cut to 46" billets and must be planted soon after. Seeds by comparison are easy to store and transport, can be planted with existing equipment designs, and can be planted with the degree of specificity and accuracy associated with modern agronomic practices.

Of course, hemp varieties that produce cannabinoids represent a co-product market of significant scale and economic potential. The current environment of state-level legalization and federal permissiveness has already spurred hemp cultivation in Colorado and Washington, which itself will lead to the development of additional co-products as well as improvements in agricultural practices.

What remains to be seen is whether a critical mass of development is allowed to take hold, whereby legal certainty and an everincreasing variety of enduses spurs the commoditization of the hemp plant.

This would be a situation much like for corn today. Corn is a staple crop and corn stover is a candidate for making ethanol because each of corn's components find multiple enduses.

Whereas corn is valorized by separating out each fraction of the kernel, much the same can be envisioned for hemp. Over time and with sufficient scale, optimum yield practices will emerge relative to market demand for each of hemp's subfractions. While some seeds would certainly be needed for replanting, the majority could be crushed into oils and animal feeds. This would leave the fiber as a coproduct, altering the economics in favor of converting it into fuels, paper or textiles.

In the end, there are no technical barriers to the use of industrial hemp as a feed for the production of fuels. Likewise, the economic potential of generating fuels from hemp is in-line with other varieties of lignocellulosic biomass under consideration as agricultural commodities. Although the overall economics of biomass-derived fuels remain dependent on government subsidies, of the potential alternatives, hemp has esteemable advantages as a feedstock.

References

A. F. Mustafa, J. J. McKinnon, D. A. Christensen. The nutritive value of hemp meal for ruminants. Canadian Journal of Animal Science. 1999. 79(1): 9195.

R. Kalmendal, Hemp seed cake fed to broilers. Thesis, SLU. Swedish University of Agricultural Sciences Department of Animal Nutrition and Management Uppsala. 2008.

J. Mourot, M. Guillevic. Effect of introducing hemp oil into feed on the nutritional quality of pig meat. Oilseeds and Fats Crops and Lipids. Volume 22, Number 6, 2015.

M. Saif Ur Rehmana, N. Rashida, A. Saifd, T. Mahmoodd, J. Hana. Potential of bioenergy production from industrial hemp (Cannabis sativa): Pakistan perspective. Renewable and Sustainable Energy Reviews. Volume 18, February 2013, Pages 211 245.

T. R. Fortenbery, M. Bennett. Opportunities for Commercial Hemp Production. Review of Agricultural Economics. Volume 26, Number 1, 2004, Pages 97 117.

Feasibility of Industrial Hemp Production in the United States Pacific Northwest. Station Bulletin 681 Oregon State University Agricultural Experiment Station. May 1998.

S. Aducci, M. Errani, G Venturi. Response of Hemp to Plant Population and Nitrogen Fertilisation. Italian Journal of Agronomy. 6, 2, Pages 103 111.

B. Siposa, E. Kreugerb, S.E. Svenssonc, K. Réczeya, L. Björnssonb, G. Zacchid, Steam pretreatment of dry and ensiled industrial hemp for ethanol production, Biomass and Bioenergy, Volume 34, Issue 12, December 2010, Pages 1721 1731.

M. Kuglarza, I. Gunnarssonb, S.E. Svenssonc, T. Pradec, E. Johanssond, Irini Angelidaki. Ethanol production from industrial hemp: Effect of combined dilute acid/steam pretreatment and economic aspects. Bioresource Technology. Volume 163, July 2014, Pages 236–243.

Alarua M., Kukkc L., Oltb J., Menindb A., Lauka R., Vollmera E., Astoverc A.; Lignin content and briquette quality of different fibre hemp plant types and energy sunflower; Field Crops Research. Volume 124, Issue 3, 20 December 2011, Pages 332–339

The Lakota Hemp Development Effort at Pine Ridge

Kurt Siedschlaw, MS,JD

Professor of Criminal Justice, University of Nebraska Keaney

Many historians use the death of Crazy Horse in September 1877 at Fort Robinson Nebraska as the symbolic end to the Sioux Wars that had started in 1854. The systematic slaughter of millions of bison and the relentless military campaign against the Lakota Sioux and their Cheyenne and Arapaho allies brought a sudden end to the Horse Culture that had dominated the northern Great Plains for two hundred years. Never actually defeated, the Lakota Sioux agreed to return to established reservations after negotiation with the federal government. Though located within the boundaries of the United States and South Dakota, the Pine Ridge Lakota are a sovereign nation. Many of the tribal elders sought to hold tight to traditional ways while knowing the tribe must interact with the AngloEuropean culture.

Life on the reservation was difficult, with every aspect of the traditional culture facing extreme stress. The Lakota faced low life expectancy, rampant unemployment, wrenching poverty, and high levels of substance abuse. The continued existence of the culture was in jeopardy. Federal policy aimed to force assimilation into the broader American society. One of the most destructive aspects of federal policy dealt with land ownership. In 1887, Congress passed the General Allotment Act (also known as the Dawes Act), which authorized the president to divide reservation land into allotments for Native American families. This would force the once nomadic people to become settled farmers and would separate tribes into individual landowners to break up the traditional tribal way of life. However, the Dawes Act created a substantial barrier to economic development. Over time, as land ownership passed down through inheritance, it created a situation where reservation lands have become severely fractioned. This has created a management nightmare where a project may require the signed approval of dozens, hundreds or even thousands of separate land owners.

The Oglala Lakota Nation of the Pine Ridge Reservation in southwestern South Dakota originally consisted of approximately 2.7 million acres, roughly the size of Connecticut. Today, of the remaining 1,773,760 acres of land, nearly 1,067,877 acres (60%) is allotted to individuals. Most of these acres have

Lakota chiefs and U.S. officials at Pine Ridge, 1891

multiple owners. As a result of this ownership complexity, tribal land owners have few choices except to lease their lands out as part of the Bureau of Indian Affairs range management unit leasing system.   This system is run by the federal government not by the tribe, which has resulted in the land often being leased to nontribal interests. Many individual tribal land owners end up with annual checks for a few dollars.

An effort was initiated in the mid-1990s to reclaim local control over the allotted land. Several families incorporated their collective family land interests into a land use corporation. In the spring of 1997, Tom Cook, a Native American Community Activist and Joe American Horse, a political leader of the Lakota Nation, held a meeting near Chadron, Nebraska to discuss economic development and a plan to establish a functional land use association. Along with the leaders the meeting included several traditional elders from Pine Ridge, my teenage son, and me.

I was invited because I am an attorney and a university professor with a background in working with tribes on economic development, discrimination, and overrepresentation of Native Americans in the justice system. My son was there because children are an important part of Lakota culture. His attendance with me was important to the tribal elders, because it signified the inclusion of the upcoming generation, a strong cultural tradition of the Lakota.

Photo courtesy of Peter Schweitzer

This upcoming generation is referred to as the 7th Generation, which has great significance for the tribe. The meeting was a forward looking and innovative effort by the local people to affirm their independence and political sovereignty, improve their economic selfsufficiency, and preserve their culture.

Joe American Horse, Tom Cook and his wife Loretta Afraid of Bear have worked for decades to improve the condition of the people of the Pine Ridge. Before the meeting began, attendees shared a sweat lodge experience, one of the central rituals of the Lakota culture. This ritual prepared those in attendance to speak clearly, openly and honestly about the issues at hand. The sweat lodge ceremony included two hours in a totally dark lodge similar in size to a small igloo. A pit in the middle of the earthen floor was filled with superheated rocks, and water was sprinkled on the rocks to create steam. The cleansing of the sweat lodge was followed by a meal and then the matters of interest were discussed. One of the topics was the potential of industrial hemp cultivation on the Pine Ridge Reservation as a tool of economic development.

Industrial Hemp as an Economic Development Effort

After reviewing the existing governmental and university reports evaluating the potential of industrial hemp as a viable agricultural product, Joe American Horse and Tom Cook submitted a proposal to the Pine Ridge Tribal Council. The Tribal Council then passed a tribal ordinance on July 28th 1998: *The Oglala Sioux Tribe: Law and Order Code: No. 98 – 27*, which authorized the cultivation of industrial hemp product on the reservation and clearly distinguished industrial hemp from marijuana. Alex White Plume, a Pine Ridge resident and tribal member, was selected by the Tribal Council to manage the first hemp project on tribal lands within the sovereign nation of the Oglala Lakota.

In the spring of 2000, Alex White Plume, under the authority of the enacted ordinance, planted one and one half acres with certified industrial hemp seed imported from Canada. On August 24, 2000 a task force of 36 Drug Enforcement Administration, FBI, U.S. Marshals and Bureau of Indian Affairs law enforcement officers raided the farm, cut down and removed the mature crop that was ready to be harvested the following week. The pattern was repeated in 2001 and 2002. None of the government raids resulted in collecting anything but very low grade (less than 1% THC content) samples that would not qualify for prosecution under federal drug laws. No arrests resulted from the raids.

Hemp Crop Destroyed but Endeavor Continues

Even as Alex White Plume was seeing his crops destroyed, the Slim Butts Land Use Association quietly proceeded to build a house on the reservation with the primary construction material produced from industrial hemp. The destruction of the local crop forced the association to import hemp from Canada. Five house materials were made from hemp: the wall hempcrete blocks, fiber insulation, hempcrete wall panels, hemp fiber in the exterior stucco, and hemp shingles. Aided by a $60,000 grant from Anita Roddick, the association built the wood frame, made 2,000 hempcrete blocks and imported fifty-year warrantee hemp shingles from Canada. Ms. Roddick is the founder of The Body Shop, a British cosmetics company that was an early pioneer in the development of hempbased personal care products.

In 2004, Alex White Plume was enjoined by the Federal Court from ever attempting to grow industrial hemp. In 2016, he is still seeking a lifting of the injunction. Recent legislative actions at the national level and in several states, now create some hope for this to happen in the near future. The 2014 Farm Bill created a federally-recognized distinction between hemp and marijuana, and allowed states to enact legislation legalizing hemp cultivation for research purposes. Several states have moved more aggressively than the federal government, with hemp cultivation now legal in twelve states, and research legalized in many other states.

Members of the Lakota Nation on the Pine Ridge Reservation in South Dakota had the insight and took the initiative in 1999 to explore the potential of industrial hemp development. The United States government attempted to roadblock their efforts. The members of the Lakota Nation build a house using primarily industrial hemp products. The general

Hemp House at Slim Buttes
Photo courtesy of Peter Schweitzer

population of the United States, through the ongoing changes in federal and state legislation may soon be able to do what the Lakota people began attempting more than a decade and a half ago. There are things that can be learned from the Lakota in regard to industrial hemp and the potential of industrial hemp for lawful and constructive purposes.

Suggested Readings:

Broydo, Leora, *The Drug War Comes to the Rez*, Mother Jones, Feb. 13, 2001

Ecoffey, Brandon, *Alex White Plume Continues Hemp Battle*, Lakota Country Times, Aug. 19, 2015.

Hoover, Elizabeth, Slim Buttes Agricultural Project, Pine Ridge Reservation, http://gardenwarriorsgoodseeds.com, Dec 18, 2014

Oglala Sioux Tribe: *Law and Order Code: Ordinance No. 9827*, National Indian Law Library, Native American Rights Fund.

Scherer, Mark R., *The Dawes Act*, The Encyclopedia of the Great Plains, University of Nebraska Lincoln.

Hemp on the Farm

– A Personal Vision

We know how to grow wheat on an industrial scale. It is time to allow farmers to also grow hemp.

Hemp: Connecting Our Pioneering Past with a Sustainable Future

Deb Palm-Egle
Fourth Generation owner of a ranch that straddles the Wyoming-Nebraska Border

By 1886 the Union Pacific Railroad had wound its way west carrying with it many a man and woman who dreamed of finding something bigger, building something better for themselves and their families. When Gust Palm stepped off that train, in what would soon come to be known as the state of Wyoming, he couldn't have known that the land he would homestead would one day be my home, that he was staking a claim not only in his own future and that of his family, but in the future of an industry that had yet to even be imagined. It is because of the risk he took all those years ago, that I can stand here ready to take one of my own.

Gust Palm was my great-grandfather and far from a passive farmer lacking ambition. Having traveled halfway across the world from Sweden, he had no intention of wasting the opportunities this new beginning had to offer. He disembarked the train in Pine Bluffs with his brother and cousin, walked twenty miles and started building. What began as little more than a mud hut surrounded by rich soil, would soon grow into a house to hold a family and a farm to feed his dreams.

His son Edwin was raised with the same drive and together they raised cattle and culti-vated wheat, selling and trading until they had enough to buy a ranch. The Palm Live-stock Company ranch at Elk Mountain, Wyoming would grow into one of the largest contiguous ranches in America. These are the men of my family whose legacy taught me to trust my instincts and follow the fair winds onto new horizons, stake my claim and build.

While many of those families who made their way west all those years ago, have moved on, our farm is still there, the house he built still standing. When my father passed away, he entrusted it to me knowing I'd safeguard it, continuing to work the land and keep it in our family. I plan to do just that, and like those who have come before me, I don't intend to settle with what was left to me. I intend to grow.

I'm far from the typical wheat farmer my father was and with the inheritance of this land I see a similar opportunity Gust saw to take on a challenge, to build something I firmly believe in and leave the world a bit different for having done it. I look back at the days when hemp grew naturally on our land, unbidden but not unwelcome. That is, until the federal government decided we'd all be better off without it and banned it in 1937. Now 80 years later, the microphone has been handed to the right people, the media has shined a light and people are taking a real look at hemp for the first time.

As we're beginning to discover the

Building a house and a prosperous life on the family farm

copious benefits this plant can have in the world around us – from being used as a supplement in concrete or as a more efficient fiber with which to make paper to radical medical breakthroughs – I look at how it can also benefit the ground beneath our feet. It is a plant that in the growing of it naturally yields nutrients that the soil imbibes. Its texture can help repel certain insects that are posing a threat to wheat crops across the country. As a farmer, you can't ask for a much better crop than that; one that gives not only after harvest, but even as it grows.

I've known for some time the benefits of this plant and its cousins. You see, I've had multiple sclerosis for over thirty years. After spending too many of those years relying on western medicine's relatively ineffective attempts to treat my condition, I turned to medicinal marijuana to supplement my treatment. Since adding it to my life, not only do I feel better on a daily basis, but the progression of my M.S. has drastically slowed.

Shortly after realizing just how extraordinary this plant is, did I begin researching everything I could about cannabis and hemp from its history to its potential future. The research is still in its infancy and I'm always amazed, yet hardly surprised, when a new use is discovered. It's been around for thousands of years, but we're only beginning to tap into it's potential. I want to stand at the forefront of this emerging industry, just as my great-grandfather stood at the starting line of modern American farming.

This is where I'm staking my claim, and not just for the sake of my farm, but for every-one who has the potential to benefit. I've had many a conversation with people fighting for their lives and their health, harboring a sense of helplessness, just wanting a modicum of relief. They think there's nothing out there for them, nothing they can do to heal, that they're just waiting. But I know there is something for them. I also know that change is needed not only in regards to the actual treatment being offered, but

the attitudes around that treatment. In developing the hemp plant and industry, in funding its growth and research, I believe it will give a chance for these people to take back ownership of their health and no longer live at the mercy of modern medicine.

The wild west may have been tamed, but I still find myself on a train headed towards the horizon of possibility, very much a woman on a new frontier.

My father was a wheat grower. I want to improve on his legacy by bringing hemp to our farm.

PHOTO CREDITS

Allan Jenkins

5, 8, 9, 12, 21a, 21b, 25, 26, 28, 31, 34, 35, 36, 39, 40, 45, 46, 48, 49, 54, 56, 57, 58, 61, 63a (bird), 64, 68, 71, 80, 81, 82, 85, 86, 88, 91b, 92, 94, 95, 96, 98, 102, 103, 104, 108b, 109, 110, 112, 116, 117, 121, 122, 131, back cover

Shane Davis

6, 16, 18b, 22b, 38, 41, 47, 50, 51, 52, 55, 59, 60, 62, 63b, 65, 69, 72, 73, 74, 76, 77, 78, 79, 87, 90, 93, 97, 105, 106, 111, 118, 119, 120, 125, 126, 130

Allison Jenkins

107a, 108a

Larry Carstenson

42, 43, 44

Deb Palm-Egle

132, 133, 134

Shutter Stock

10a, 10b, 11a, 11b, 13, 14, 15a, 15b, 17, 18a, 19, 22a, 23, 24, 30, 32, 33, 66, 67, 83, 89, 91a (seeds), 99, 107b, 113, 114, 115, 127

Peter Schweitzer

128, 129

The Editor, early June in the Platte Valley: Photo by Gary Lingle